THE REMINISCENCE QUIZ BOOK

MIKE SHERMAN

Speechmark Publishing Ltd

The author would like to express his appreciation for the support and patience of Angela Tustin in the compilation of the book.

Published by
Speechmark Publishing Ltd, 70 Alston Drive, Bradwell Abbey,
Milton Keynes MK13 9HG, United Kingdom
Tel: +44 (0) 1908 326 944   Fax: +44 (0) 1908 326 960
www.speechmark.net

002-0819/Printed in the United Kingdom by Hobbs

British Library Cataloguing in Publication Data
Sherman, Mike
   The reminiscence quiz book
   1. History
   I. Title
   907.6

ISBN: 978 0 86388 352 1

CONTENTS

Mike Sherman is a graduate of Hull University. He has extensive experience of the educational requirements of special needs groups. Since specializing in the care of dementia sufferers he has been responsible for the management and development of a day centre for the seriously confused elderly which specializes in the provision of innovative stimulation pursuits. As a consequence Mike Sherman has been instrumental in the design of orientation and reminiscence aids. He is currently Chief Executive of the Association for Carers of the Elderly Confused.

Acknowledgements

Front cover photographs reproduced with kind permission from Hulton Deutsch Collection Limited; This is the BBC and No Pictures.

The *Reminiscence Quiz Book* will be of use and enjoyable for all groups of older people, not only the confused elderly. One of its main features is flexibility, allowing the level of discussion to be adjusted to the needs and abilities of the groups and individuals involved. This quality can be used to provide extra guidance when talking with confused elderly people. It can also be used to prolong and deepen discussion with other groups of older people. I have tested several parts of the book with groups of varying capabilities and found that it stimulates discussion amongst elderly people of all levels of ability. In this book I have tried to provide more than a simple list of questions and answers. Such a restricted format very often results in either an awkward silence, as questions prove too difficult, or an activity which is over too quickly as people rapidly supply the correct answers.

My main aim has been to provide a 'quiz' which will generate discussion through reminiscence either with individuals or in groups. The focus is not only on the major milestones of history, but on the matters of everyday experience. Most of the questions and answers supplied are accompanied by a certain amount of related information. This has been included to enable whoever is the 'quiz leader' to use the quiz as a means of stimulating personal memories and opinions about the topics covered.

Illustration

1942   *Daily Life*

What was supposed to be no more than five inches deep from this year?

Bathwater

Keeping clean was becoming more difficult. The fuel shortage meant that people were urged to take fewer baths and to run no more than five inches of water. Lines were painted on baths in hotels and public baths to show this level. Bathwater was frequently shared. To make things more difficult, soap was rationed (one tablet every four weeks). In 1944, *Lifebuoy* Toilet Soap was being advertised at 3½d (thruppence ha'penny) per tablet, together with one coupon. Razor blades were even harder to obtain and men tried to make them last by running them around the rim of a glass tumbler.

From the original question the quiz leader is able to develop a number of supplementary ones. These can be straightforward general enquiries or questions on more specific information. In this example, follow-up questions might include: Did you have to take fewer baths? Did you have to share the bathwater? Who had the water first? Was soap rationed? How much soap were you allowed? How much did soap cost? (Remember, information on prices, etc varies according to area and make of product.) How many coupons did it take? Were razor blades in short supply? Did you have to make them last?

If the quiz leader is successful in stimulating conversation, then much of the supplementary information (and a lot more) will follow before any encouragement is needed.

An important feature of this book is its flexibility. The extent to which the group leader uses follow-up information and the type of cues they choose depends very much upon their own judgement of the needs and abilities of the individual elderly people involved. In most cases, a question's level of difficulty is not fixed, as the supplementary information can be used to offer a range of clues to the answer. This provides an opportunity to adjust questions to people rather than fit people into an inappropriate pre-set format.

How to use the book

Questions cover a number of areas. A proportion concentrate on aspects of daily life, while others involve more conventional quiz subjects — entertainment, people and news. Wherever possible I have included personalities who, though not often featured in modern accounts of the period, were well known at the time. 'Old Mother Riley' (Arthur Lucan) and Frank Randle of the 1930s would fall into this category.

Questions are arranged in decades, each of which includes a variety of clearly marked topic areas. I have adopted this format to avoid the boredom which can be produced when group members are uninterested in specific subjects. It also provides the flexibility of being able to offer an individual a choice of the remaining subject areas without having to flick around sections.

Above all, I hope that the *Reminiscence Quiz Book* will provide entertainment to many older people. I am also confident that it will prove of interest to those acting as quiz leader. The book has been designed to supply a painless learning process for anyone who has regular contact with older people. By leading this simple, social activity, a younger person can build up a store of information which will prove useful in any reminiscence activity or in everyday conversation.

Age Awareness

These are guidelines which need to be considered before and during any reminiscence activity.

1 Age Appropriateness

It is a simple failing of much reminiscence work that little attention is paid to the implications of an elderly person's age.

"How old is the person I am talking to?" This basic question provides the key to relevant reminiscence. Its most obvious implication is, "Are they old enough to remember this event?" It is surprising how often people are asked to recall incidents from a year they could not reasonably be expected to remember. How much can you remember of life when you were four?

2 Age Association

With a little practice and by acquiring a small amount of information, reminiscence leaders can introduce specific events which complement a person's life history.

If Alice was married in 1936, you might comment: "That was the year King Edward abdicated, wasn't it?" If the marriage was in 1939: "Didn't the war begin that year?" If her son was born in 1948, you might ask: "Wasn't that the same year that the Queen had Prince Charles?" Perhaps Bill retired in 1966: "Were you still at work when England won the World Cup?"

This approach illustrates an important feature of reminiscence work. The most meaningful way of remembering events is through association with a person's own life history. By using the marker points of a confused person's own life, we can help them to become more aware of the passage of time. For example it can be pointed out to Alice that the abdication took place when she was a young bride. This helps to remind Alice that her wedding day was a long time ago and that she is now an elderly lady. Since the abdication, we have had George VI (the Queen's father) and the present Queen, who is now over 60, on the throne.

If you are working with confused elderly people, the practice of age-association can prove valuable in reality orientation. A correct perception of age and date is of great importance in clearing the confusion of an

84-year-old lady who claims still to have small children or who wants to go home to her parents.

3 Age, attitude and feeling

Memories are not only a recording of past events but also reflect people's different life stages. An elderly man has, typically, also seen life as a young boy, an unattached young man, a young husband, the father of small children and a responsible middle-aged man.

Each stage has greatly affected his attitudes and outlook. Try to see a person's life in stages and in relation to the other members of the group. What would they be interested in and experience at each life stage? Age is not simply a matter of accumulating years but of changing roles.

A woman born in 1929 would be 10 in 1939. This means that she will have seen the start of the Second World War through the eyes of a small girl. Perhaps she was excited and frightened by the experience of evacuation. A woman born in 1901 would be 38 in 1939. She could have seen the same event through the eyes of a worried mother, whose 18-year-old son would soon be eligible to be called up.

Any reminiscence work should involve more than just the recollection of facts. Nostalgia is incomplete if it does not include the expression of emotions. Without this, reminiscence will become emotionally sterile. Feeling is an essential part of everyone's recollections. Memories of events as varied as a wedding day and the Blitz are much more meaningful if the person recalls the feelings produced by the experience.

4 Reminiscence and opinion

Whatever subject is being covered in a reminiscence session, the group involved will almost certainly have a variety of opinions about it. These opinions can cover simple matters of taste, as when you are talking about a film star. Facts about the titles of films and the names of co-stars are important, but they are supplementary to the basic question, "Did you like her?" If someone thinks that George Formby was awful, they should be encouraged to say so.

The most animated reminiscence sessions are often those where the group disagrees on a subject. Leaders should take care to remember that public figures or politicians who now seem simply to be quaint figures from the past could easily have been very controversial people when they were alive. Members of the group could well have had strongly held opinions about them.

the 1930s

THE **1930s** are seen in popular memory as a bleak decade, characterized by unemployment and poverty. This picture is only appropriate for part of the country. Areas such as the North-East, northern England and South Wales did struggle through much of the decade. These were regions which had depended largely on Britain's traditional 'heavy' industries, such as shipbuilding, coal mining and cotton, industries which entered a long-term decline between the two world wars. Each was to lose approximately one third of its workforce. Cotton fell from third place to eleventh in importance to British industry.

Unemployment due to the Depression at the start of the 1930s reached a peak of three million in January 1933. It was to fall by 500,000 in the same year as recovery came, but when the decade ended one million were still out of work. Towns such as Wigan, Bolton, Jarrow and Colne saw the worst of this.

At the same time as Britain's heavy industries declined, there was a boom in industries which produced goods and services for the home market. The Electricity Supply Industry increased its consumers from three quarters of a million in 1920 to nine million in 1938. Almost three million houses were built in the 1930s. These developments brought an increase in the demand for electrical equipment, radio sets and new furniture, a demand encouraged by the arrival of hire-purchase. Most electrical appliances were still only owned by a minority but their numbers were growing. Irons were the most common, while the number of vacuum cleaners produced increased more than ten-fold between 1930 and 1935. Refrigerators were still very rare.

There were nine million wireless sets licensed by the end of the decade, as against three million in 1930. In a pre-television age, the radio occupied a central place, bringing entertainment and information directly into the home for the first time. The 1930s saw a better-informed public. Concurrent with the expansion of radio, mass newspaper readerships developed (in 1933 the *Daily Express* and the *Daily Herald* had achieved circulations of over two million).

The boom which was produced by the new industries benefited southern England and parts of the Midlands. The old industries had been sited near raw materials and ports. The new factories used electricity and road transport. Owners were mainly concerned to have their factories sited near large, prosperous population centres. Many yielded to the attraction of

London and established themselves in the South-East. Even in the bleakest years of the Depression, unemployment in an area like Middlesex was only 5 per cent and under. This created two nations in Britain: the booming areas of southern England and the northern areas blighted by long-term unemployment. People's experience of the 1930s can therefore be very different. The image of poverty and a dour struggle with the means test in the back-to-backs will mean little to a middle-class couple who had their new semi at Oxford or Bletchley.

A large number of men from the depressed regions simply moved to where the newer industries were providing work. Any group of elderly people in what was a 1930s boom town, such as Coventry, will be varied and almost certainly include a large number from the blighted areas such as the North-East, South Wales and parts of Scotland. A fruitful subject of conversation is individual memories of the often traumatic move that was necessary.

Outside the home, the biggest entertainment was the cinema. In 1934 the average weekly audience was 18.4 million. The start of the decade had coincided with the coming of sound. During the 1930s a new type of 'super cinema' began to appear, in which audiences could watch the latest Hollywood extravaganza in ornately splendid surroundings. They were often given suitably glamorous names, such as the Astoria, Rialto, Roxy or Ritz. The new cinemas also provided an element of escape and privacy to people who might be living in crowded, run-down housing.

There were other signs that more people were enjoying themselves, despite the gloom imposed upon some areas. Many more were taking holidays by 1939. These were generally spent at the popular seaside resorts. By 1939, 11 million had even secured holidays with pay.

Much attention is also often paid to the 1930s and the 'drift towards war'. For the purposes of reminiscence, this is again a misrepresentation. We are often guilty of equating the historical significance of events with a general awareness. This is not necessarily the case. The Munich Agreement of 1938 is an example. Munich's importance is due to what happened in subsequent years. At the time, it was seen by many as an argument between foreigners over a place very few people had ever heard of (the Sudetenland region of Czechoslovakia). People did not know that a world war would soon break out.

What happened to the world's largest airship on 4 October?

It crashed

On its maiden flight to India, the R101 exploded in a fireball and hit a hillside near Beauvais in France. Forty-four people were killed when the five-and-a-half million cubic feet of hydrogen on board ignited. The R101 disaster marked the end of major British involvement in airships. The R101 was not the first British airship disaster. The potential dangers had been revealed when the R38 had crashed into the river Humber near Hull, killing 43, in 1921.

Name the woman who made a 10,000-mile solo flight to Australia with only 100 hours' flying experience and in a second-hand aircraft.

Amy Johnson

The 1930s were the great age of record breaking and achievement in flight and speed. Johnson was the daughter of a Hull fish merchant who became a national heroine with her flying adventures. She was the first woman to make the solo flight to Australia. Press reports described her flying through sandstorms, making forced landings and patching up the wings of her Gypsy Moth with sticking plaster. In 1932 Amy Johnson married another well-known flier, Jim Mollinson. The marriage was dissolved in 1938.

What happened to speed record holder Sir Henry Seagrave on Friday 13 June?

He was killed in a crash

Seagrave crashed his 4,000 hp motor boat, *Miss England II* on Lake Windermere after it had struck a floating obstacle. Moments before he had achieved a new world's water speed record of 98.76 mph. Both Seagrave and his mechanic, Halliwell, were killed (an engineer survived). Seagrave was also well-known for his motor racing exploits.

What was the line of defences which the French government announced in October that it was to begin to build?

The Maginot Line

What sort of animal was Larry in Toytown?

A lamb

Larry the Lamb was a character in the *Toytown* series which was part of the BBC's *Children's Hour*. Other *Toytown* characters included Dennis the Dachshund, Ernest the Policeman, The Mayor of Toytown and Mr Growserr. *Toytown* was narrated by Derek McCulloch (Uncle Mac) who also played the leading character of Larry the Lamb. It was Uncle Mac who coined the phrase, 'Goodnight children, everywhere', later to be used as a song title. *Children's Hour* also featured stories, talks, plays and competitions read by a variety of Radio uncles and aunts. McCulloch became Head of Children's Broadcasting in 1933. A small innovation made by him was to introduce a signature tune to *Children's Hour*, using an old musical box.

Who scored a record 334 runs in the third Test Match at Leeds in July?

Don Bradman

The young Australian broke several batting records during this test series. His 288th run established the highest individual test innings. This stood until 1938, when Yorkshire batsman Len Hutton scored 364 runs for England. Bradman played in the same Test Match but fell and broke a shin bone. Before his cricketing exploits, Bradman had been a farm worker near Sydney. The Australian had made a world's record score of 452 not out in 1929.

Who was the beautiful film star from Sweden who began to talk in the movie Anna Christie?

Greta Garbo

Garbo had begun her film career in Sweden in 1924. She made a succession of silent films in Hollywood during the 1920s. She was one of the few screen stars who made a successful transition to sound films. Many others were found to have totally unsuitable voices for the new format. Garbo's last silent film was *The Kiss* (1929). Her move into talkies with *Anna Christie* was publicized with the slogan, 'Garbo Talks'. The early 1930s saw the talkies produce their first generation of stars. Other well-known films made by Garbo included: *Mata Hari* (1932), *Queen Christina* (1933), *Anna Karenina* (1935), *Camille* (1936) and *Ninotchka* (1939). Her male co-stars included John Gilbert and Robert Taylor.

What was Weldon's Catalogue?

A popular magazine for housewives (it included patterns)

What did a housewife use a 'dolly' for?

Washing clothes

Although washing machines were available, these were both crude and uncommon. The spread of electricity during the 1930s (the National Grid was completed in 1935) made machines more practicable for those able to afford them, though these were very much a minority of the population. Washday produced much physical work for the housewife or maid involved (many more young women worked in domestic service at the time). If there was no washing machine, the dolly was used to agitate the clothes. The wooden dolly resembled a milking-stool on a pole. Using much physical effort, the housewife would move its wooden prongs back and forth in the washing. Hot water had to be boiled in a copper and bar soap, along with *Rinso* and *Borax*, was used to scrub the washing. Excess water was removed with a mangle.

Who were the 'number please' girls?

Telephone operators

On early telephones, callers were not connected automatically, by dialling a number, but by an operator. London's first automatic telephone exchange had been installed in 1927, at Holborn. Automatic exchanges and 'autophones' rapidly replaced the 'number please' girls. By 1933 more than half of London's calls were being handled by automatic exchanges. Though its use was spreading, the telephone was still comparatively rare. In 1933 there were 274,000 new installations made.

How old did you have to be to hold a motor-cycle driving licence at the start of 1930?

Fourteen

One of several changes introduced in the Road Traffic Act of December 1930 was to raise the minimum age for holding a motor-cycle licence to 16. Very few young lads had the money to afford anything more than small, low-powered machines (such as a 150 cc Francis-Barnett). They would move up to something more substantial as they got older and began to earn more.

What was 'Marcel Waving' or 'Eugene Waving'?

Permanent waving (having a 'perm')

Who was the star of the movie Mammy?

Al Jolson

Jolson was a stage and screen star of the late 1920s and 1930s. The title *Mammy* was taken from one of his most famous songs and featured him in his best-known and most characteristic role, that of a black-faced minstrel. 1930 also saw Jolson appear in *Big Boy*, which again included many popular songs. Other 1930s films included *Wonder Bar* (1934), *The Singing Kid* (1936) and *Rose of Washington Square* (1939). Jolson is most often associated with his role in *The Jazz Singer* (1927). This was the film which paved the way for the 'talkies'. Only the songs were supposed to be recorded, but Jolson's continual ad-libbing while the microphones were operating made nonsense of this. After his first song he silenced the clapping extras with the famous words, "You ain't heard nothing yet." Songs included *Toot, Toot, Tootsie, Goodbye* and *Blue Skies*.

Who was the 6' 10" Italian boxer who came to London in December?

Primo Carnera

This Italian heavyweight caused a stir because of his extraordinary size. He wore size 16 shoes, 21-inch collars and had a 58-inch chest. The Press was also fascinated by his huge appetite and friendly, gentle personality. He had been a poorly-paid carpenter only a year before. Carnera came to London to fight Reggie Meen at the Albert Hall. The bout lasted only four and a half minutes before the referee awarded the fight to the giant Italian.

Name the Scotsman from Lossiemouth who was Prime Minister of the Labour Government in 1930.

James Ramsay MacDonald

MacDonald had been the Prime Minister of the first ever Labour Government in 1924. This minority government had lasted only nine months. In June 1929 he headed another Labour Government without a majority. Although he was always more interested in foreign affairs, domestic concerns were to prove decisive for MacDonald's political future. In 1931 the Labour Government collapsed when half the Cabinet were unwilling to impose severe cuts in unemployment relief, yet were unable to put forward any alternatives. MacDonald went on to lead a National Government which the Labour Party did not join. Disowned by Labour, he became a figurehead without a base of support, gaining a reputation as a traitor amongst many of the Labour Party.

Which royal spectator was present when Arsenal won the cup this year, beating Huddersfield Town 2–0?

King George V

What happened at Invergordon in September?

A mutiny

Several thousand Royal Navy sailors refused to put to sea in protest at the pay cuts imposed upon them by the new National Government. A shilling a day had been taken from all ranks, leaving some men with as little as 25s a week. Some men had only found out about the cuts when they had read about the government economy programme in the newspapers. The 'mutiny' was really a two-day strike involving very little violence. Eventually the cuts were revised on a percentage basis. The 24 ringleaders of the mutiny were dismissed from the service.

What unpopular test was imposed on the unemployed receiving long-term unemployment assistance in 1931?

The means test

The needs of unemployed people who had exhausted their contributions had become a topical issue. The means test was introduced as one of the economies of 1931. It was carried out by the public assistance committees of local councils and was one of the decade's most controversial issues. The test sought to discover whether families had any 'means' which could be taken into account before giving benefit.

The extensive Welfare State we are accustomed to was not available in the 1930s. Many people thought it wrong that a man should receive relief if they had resources of their own. Conversely others felt it unfair that a man should be penalized for being provident before unemployment or because other members of his family were in work. The 'snooping' involved in the test also caused great ill-feeling.

What happened to the submarine HMS Poseidon on 9 June?

It sank after a collision

The *Poseidon* was exercising in the China Sea when it surfaced too close to the steamer *Yuta*. The submarine was badly damaged and sank in only two minutes. A total of 31 men scrambled clear, leaving 24 trapped. Six of these men were grouped by Petty Officer Willis in the vessel's bows. With the aid of new escape apparatus they managed to squeeze out of their flooding compartment after three and a half hours. The other 18 men were trapped behind water-tight doors in other parts of the submarine.

Which government gained a large vote of confidence in their October General Election victory?

The National Government

Who was the glamorous platinum blonde movie star who wanted to "slip into something more comfortable"?

Jean Harlow

Harlow made a succession of films in the early 1930s. These included *Blonde Bombshell* (1933), *Dinner at Eight* (1933) and *China Seas* (1935). She made this well-known remark in an earlier movie, *Hell's Angels* (1930). Her most frequent leading man was Clark Gable (as in *Red Dust*, in 1932). Harlow's personal life was turbulent. She had three husbands, none for very long. In 1937 she died from a kidney disease, aged 26. Her last film, *Saratoga*, was completed by a double. A morbid public flocked to the movie to see if they could spot where the stand-in took over.

For which non-speaking part is Boris Karloff best remembered?

Frankenstein's monster

During the early 1930s, Universal Studios were famous for their horror films. Their two best-known horror movie creations were Frankenstein's monster and Dracula. Englishman Boris Karloff was the monster in *Frankenstein* (1931). The bloodsucking, Transylvanian Count was played by the Hungarian actor Bela Lugosi in *Dracula* (1931). Many other actors have since played both these parts. Other 1930s horror films introduced *The Invisible Man* (1933), *The Mummy* (1932) and *The Bride of Frankenstein* (1935).

What well-known song did Marlene Dietrich sing in the film The Blue Angel?

Falling in Love Again

Dietrich was a star of the first decade of talkies. Her films included *Morocco* (1930) with Gary Cooper, *Shanghai Express* (1932) as Shanghai Lily and *Blonde Venus* (1932) with Cary Grant. These films established Dietrich's glamorous *femme fatale* image. She would often be swathed in furs and had a distinctive, deep voice.

Who were the comic singing duo that featured songs such as Big Ben Calling *and* Weather Reports *on radio shows such as* Our Hour *and* Signs of the Times?

Flotsam and Jetsam

What type of transport was powered by overhead cables in the street but did not run on tracks?

The trolley bus

These were the trackless trams which took over from trams in several cities during the 1920s and 1930s. Tramlines had reached their fullest development in 1928. However, as tracks became due for renewal, operators began to switch to trolleys which were cheaper and did not interfere as much with other traffic. Trolleys ended the dominance of the tram but were themselves gradually replaced by the motor-bus which had even greater mobility. The motor-bus was able to continue out of a city rather than have to stop where the cables ended. Trolleys had made their debut in Yorkshire. By 1931 regular trolley-bus services had begun in some districts of London.

What began to be drawn, three times a year, from a huge drum which stood in the Plaza Cinema Hall, Dublin?

The Irish Sweepstake

Public lotteries were forbidden in England. However the Irish government allowed the sweepstake to be established, on condition that it gave a large part of its proceeds to Irish hospitals. The British postal authorities could not prevent people from buying tickets in Dublin without interfering with the mail. Hundreds of thousands of tickets were therefore sold to British gamblers and during the 1930s the Sweepstake collected £60 million, of which it gave £14 million to Irish hospitals. The Sweepstake was first run in 1930 on the Manchester Handicap, but in 1931 it was extended to three races: the Grand National, the Derby and the Cesarewitch.

What was the speed limit in built-up areas in this year?

There wasn't one

In 1930 the obsolete speed limit of 20 mph had been abolished. For the next four years drivers were free from all restriction. In 1934 a limit of 30 mph was introduced for built-up areas. Roads still bore a large amount of horse-drawn traffic, especially for commercial vehicles such as delivery vans. Although speed was discouraged, the mixing of traffic and sometimes reckless driving meant accidents were numerous.

What simple, small device had just begun to save much frustrating fiddling with hook and eye?

The zip-fastener

Who was the singing star who concluded his stage act with Susie, Ma, He's Making Eyes at Me *and* Making Whoopee *in black-face medley?*

Eddie Cantor

Cantor was a stage star of the late 1920s who made a number of popular movie musicals during the 1930s. His appeal was similar to that of Al Jolson. (Cantor had sung *Yes, We Have No Bananas* in the 1920s and Jolson included it in his 1930 film, *Mammy*.) Cantor's best-known song was *Making Whoopee*, which featured in the stage show *Whoopee* and film of the same name (1930). Cantor's films were very popular (*Whoopee* grossed two and a half million dollars world-wide). 1931 saw further success with *Palmy Days*, followed by *Roman Scandals* (1933) and *Strike Me Pink* (1936). Cantor had also become America's highest paid radio star by 1936.

Who came to Buckingham Palace in November, dressed in a loin-cloth, and met the King?

Gandhi

The leading campaigner for Indian independence had come to London to attend a round-table conference which had been summoned to discuss India's future. Gandhi had not long been released from prison after leading a campaign to defy the government salt monopoly.

Ever since he had become aware of India's crushing poverty, Gandhi had worn the coarse loin-cloth of the peasant, with bare chest and legs. In order to be like the poorest of India's poor, Gandhi also went without dentures. His only luxury was a steel watch, worn pinned to his loin cloth. During his stay in England, Gandhi took accommodation in the East End of London. The prospect of the King-Emperor being confronted by a small, toothless man in a loin-cloth attracted much publicity. The conference itself was a failure, but the visit had given Gandhi a world audience for his message on Indian independence.

Whose tramp figure made a rare 1930s movie appearance in City Lights *this year?*

Charlie Chaplin

Chaplin had been a popular comedian of the silent cinema. His many films from 1915 through the 1920s had made his tramp figure known throughout the world. However the coming of the 'talkies' had made Chaplin's type of humour redundant practically overnight. There was virtually no place in the 1930s for his tramp figure, with Chaplin making only two films in the decade: *City Lights* and *Modern Times* (1936). Both had soundtracks but still made minimal use of dialogue. Neither was particularly popular. Chaplin did not fit in with what 1930s audiences wanted.

Who was the nurse heroine of this year's film Night Nurse?

Barbara Stanwyck

Where was there a serious prison mutiny in January?

Dartmoor

Three hundred convicts mutinied and, for a time, gained complete control. They set fire to buildings, destroyed prison records and raided the prison officers' canteen. Warders and specially armed police managed to regain control after fighting in which 84 prisoners were injured. Trouble had been simmering for many weeks. Complaints about prison diet were an immediate cause and conditions in the prison were very poor. It had been built in 1806 and some people now saw it as unfit for use as a jail. The 30 men tried after the mutiny received additional sentences of up to 22 years. George O'Donovan, a convicted murderer, had five years taken off his sentence for rescuing the prison governor when he was attacked during the riot.

What was the name of the steam engine which travelled from King's Cross to Edinburgh in a record 7 hours 27 minutes this year?

The Flying Scotsman

During the 1930s, crack steam engines such as the Royal Scot, Cheltenham Flyer and Mallard preserved the railways' prestige by providing record-breaking express services. The London–Edinburgh express service was covered by the Flying Scotsman in the day and then by its sister engine the Night Scotsman.

At this time, the private railway companies — London and North-Eastern Railway (LNER), Southern, London, Midland and Scottish (LMS) and Great Western — frequently campaigned for government assistance. Lack of finance meant that there was restricted investment over the decade in new rolling stock and facilities and everyday services were deteriorating noticeably. Competition grew from coaches for holiday traffic and journeys between large cities and from the delivery van and lorry.

Why did the American flyer Charles Lindbergh's 20-month-old baby son make the news in March?

He was kidnapped from Lindbergh's New Jersey mansion

Although a $50,000 ransom was paid, the kidnapper did not return the child. Despite an intensive search, the baby was not found until 73 days later, when a truck driver discovered the body in a wood five miles from Lindbergh's home. Bruno Hauptmann, a 33-year-old German–American carpenter, was arrested, tried, found guilty and finally executed for the crime (in 1936). He consistently protested his innocence, losing two appeals. Much of the evidence against him was circumstantial.

What new London headquarters did the BBC move to in May?

Broadcasting House in Portland Place

Who was Oliver Hardy's thin partner in the well-known comic double act?

Stan Laurel

Stan was born in England and emigrated to America. He began his career with 'Ollie' in the late 1920s. Laurel and Hardy were at their most popular during the early 1930s. They made 81 short films and over 20 features, such as *Our Relations* (1936). On screen, Ollie was the fat, bossy, pompous one of the pair whilst Stan played an easily bullied, bungling character.

By 1940 their films had become old-fashioned and they only made nine more, not very popular, films. Audiences wanted to see more modern comedians, such as Bob Hope. Stan Laurel had ginger hair, a fact little realized by the massive audience of filmgoers who saw him in black and white.

Who did Johnny Weismuller first appear as in this year?

Tarzan

There have been over a dozen screen Tarzans. The most famous of these is Weismuller who, before his film career, had been a very successful Olympic swimmer. He made 12 Tarzan movies between 1932 (*Tarzan the Ape Man*) and 1948 (*Tarzan and the Mermaids*). Until 1943 Tarzan's mate had been played by Maureen O'Sullivan. She and Tarzan lived in a jungle tree-house (introduced in the third film). They were joined by Boy in *Tarzan finds a Son* (1939).

Which Hollywood German Shepherd was a great favourite of the 1930s?

Rin Tin Tin

The original Rin Tin Tin died this year, having starred in 22 films and two serials during the 1920s and early 1930s. His place was taken by Rin Tin Tin II, who continued the Alsatian's adventures through the 1930s. The regular films and serials of the faithful and intelligent German Shepherd were great favourites in the Saturday matinees.

What was Paul Muni a fugitive from in a movie of this year?

A chain gang

How much was the wireless licence?

Ten shillings

Before listening to a radio, people were supposed to buy a 10s wireless licence from their local post office. These had gone on sale from November 1922. The figures for licence sales indicate how rapid was the rise of radio: 1923 – 595,496; 1930 – 3 million; 1931 – 4 million; 1932 – 5 million; 1939 – 9 million.

What form of entertainment was made legal on Sundays in this year?

Cinema-going

Sunday picture-going had been popular for some time. Half a million people now attended the cinema on the Sabbath. Opponents of Sunday activities protested against Sunday opening and the practice was caught out under the Sunday Observance Act. However a Sunday Cinemas Act was passed in 1932 which authorized Sunday opening. Ninety local authorities had allowed Sunday opening previously; new authorities were only supposed to begin Sunday opening after a local poll had taken place. Not many such polls were carried out, but Sunday opening became general during the Second World War.

Where was 'nothing over sixpence'?

Woolworths

Every High Street had its Woolworths, which aimed to cater for the many people with not a lot of money to spare. The famous slogan 'nothing over sixpence' was a little misleading in some cases. A saucepan could be bought for 6d — but only the pan. It was another 6d for the lid.

The 1930s saw the growth of multiple stores such as British Home Stores and International. However shopping was still a different experience from today: regular customers at a local grocer's would frequently have their orders taken to their houses by the delivery boy on his bicycle. There was now mass-produced cheaper clothing for both sexes. Montague Burton and the Fifty-Shilling Tailor produced suits for men and had outlets all over the country.

What happened to Piccadilly's street lighting on 9 May?

It was electrified

Who was the Leader of the BBC Dance Orchestra in this year?

Henry Hall

This well-known dance band leader hosted *Henry Hall's Guest Night* on the radio. He opened his broadcasts with the words "It's just the time for dancing" and closed them with "Here's to the next time." He led the BBC Dance Orchestra from 1932 to 1937.

Which two brothers were among the stars of the movie Grand Hotel?

John and Lionel Barrymore

Grand Hotel was unusual because of the number of stars it brought together in the one film. There were five actors with 'above title' billing: Greta Garbo, John Barrymore, Joan Crawford, Wallace Beery and Lionel Barrymore. The film portrayed the lives of a number of characters as they passed through a stylish Berlin hotel, with the plots surrounding each individual being woven together. *Grand Hotel* was much acclaimed at the time and won an Oscar for best film. Garbo plays an ageing ballerina, Grusinskaya. It is in *Grand Hotel* that she sobs, "I want to be alone."

Which American President had been paralysed in both legs by polio 10 years before he was first elected?

Franklin Delano Roosevelt

Franklin Roosevelt was a Democrat President of the United States for a record four terms (1932, 1936, 1940 and 1944). In his first term he promised a 'New Deal' to combat the mass unemployment and poverty in Depression-hit America. The 'New Deal' provided employment through public works and gave help to bankrupt farmers.

Roosevelt encouraged the US to provide help to Britain and Russia in the fight against Hitler. He was also President for the years in which America herself fought in the war (after 1941). However he was never to see the final victory, as he died in April 1945, only weeks before the German surrender.

What two parts won Frederic March a single Oscar this year?

Dr Jekyll and Mr Hyde

Which was the first daily newspaper to sell two million copies a day?

The *Daily Express*

During the 1930s newspaper owners came to realize that their newspapers now depended not on readers but on advertising revenue. The key to this revenue was larger circulation, which meant higher advertising rates. Newspapers now bought readers. This realization led to a circulation war.

The *Daily Herald* began to win readers by door-to-door canvassing. The *Daily Mail* offered free insurance to registered readers. Some dailies began to offer free gifts as inducements to new readers. Silk stockings, encyclopedias and sets of Dickens joined free insurance in the sales pitch. Each new reader cost the *Daily Express* 8s 3d (eight shillings and three pence).

Who was the Austrian corporal who became Chancellor of Germany this year?

Adolf Hitler

On Monday 30 January, Hitler presided over his first Cabinet meeting as Chancellor. He had been brought to the Chancellorship by a combination of substantial popular support and the political wheeler-dealing of German Nationalist/conservative leaders who wrongly believed that they would be able to control him once he was in office.

Another German news story was the mysterious burning of the Reichstag or Parliament. An attempt was made to hold this up as the result of a Communist plot and a young Dutch Communist, Van de Lubbe, was executed, on questionable grounds.

What reached its all-time peak of just under three million in January?

The number of registered unemployed

The unemployment total fell by 500,000 during 1933 as recovery from the Depression came, but, even when recovery was under way, nearly two million long-term unemployed persisted through the 1930s. Areas such as the North-East, South Wales and northern England were worst affected. Britain's older heavy industries, such as shipbuilding, coal mining and cotton, were in decline. These had been major employers in northern communities like Wigan, Bolton, Colne and Hartlepool. A significant number of jobless men moved to towns in the South and parts of the Midlands, where newer industries (including motor manufacturers and electrical appliance producers) provided work. During the early 1930s there were also protest marches on London by men from the distressed areas.

Which English fast bowler injured an Australian batsman in the Third Test, using the controversial bodyline bowling technique?

Harold Larwood

Who was the actor from Scarborough who starred as Henry VIII in a film of this year?

Charles Laughton

Laughton starred as some of the best-known movie tyrants and villains of the 1930s. He was Henry VIII in *The Private Life of Henry VIII* (1933), Nero in *The Sign of the Cross* (1932), Captain Bligh in *Mutiny on the Bounty* (1935) and Mr Barrett in *The Barretts of Wimpole Street* (1934). Laughton also played Quasimodo in *The Hunchback of Notre Dame* (1939).

What new radio programme began to "silence the mighty roar of London's traffic" at 7.30 on Saturday nights from 18 November?

In Town Tonight

Knightsbridge by Eric Coates was used to introduce *In Town Tonight*, which was amongst the first radio shows to use a regular theme tune. The music would blend into traffic noises, then everything stopped and listeners heard: "Once again we silence the mighty roar of London's traffic to bring to the microphone some of the interesting people who are . . . In Town Tonight." Lionel Gamlin was the first interviewer (followed by Roy Rich and Gilbert Harding in the late 1940s). Michael Standing interviewed the 'man in the street' (live) in the 'Standing on the Corner' spot. The finale came with the announcer declaring, "Carry on London" and the traffic moved again.

Who carried Fay Wray to the top of the Empire State Building?

King Kong

The film *King Kong* (1933) was the story of a giant ape. After being captured in the jungle, Kong is taken back to New York to be exhibited. He escapes and wreaks havoc in the city. In the final scene, the persecuted ape carries Wray to the top of the Empire State Building, where he is killed by fighter aircraft. King Kong was, in reality, played by a 16-inch high, animated model.

What well-known song did the three little pigs sing in Walt Disney's Oscar-winning short cartoon?

Who's Afraid Of The Big Bad Wolf?

How much was a pack of five Woodbines?

2d

Wild Woodbine was the leading, mass-produced, cheap cigarette — the 'people's cigarette'. The price had been increased to 2d in 1920 and was to stay there until 1939. Packs of 10 were available before the 1930s and 20 packs were introduced during the decade. However the pack of five was very popular because it provided a 'cheap smoke'. (The *Woodbine* pack of five ended in 1973.) The original *Woodbine* packet was a strip of paper folded around five cigarettes with only the glued edge to add strength. During the 1930s, cigarette cards were added as stiffeners. The major competitors in the cheap smoke market were *Player's Weights* and *Gallaher's Park Drive*.

What was the Mighty Wurlitzer?

A cinema organ

The Mighty Wurlitzer was a feature of the super cinemas built in the 1930s. These were big enough to seat up to 3,000 and were given glamorous names such as Majestic, Astoria, Rialto, Roxy, Granada and Ritz. The organ console rose from beneath the front of the stage while the organist began his recital of popular tunes.

In an age before television and video, the cinema provided cheap and comfortable entertainment for tens of millions during the 1930s. To complete their evening's entertainment, the audience could now enjoy one of the newly available ice-cream bricks or 'choc-ices'. (An average seat price at the time was 10d.) The new cinemas provided an element of escape and privacy to many couples living in overcrowded, run-down housing.

Who were known as Nippies?

The waitresses at Lyons Corner Houses

The Lyons organization set up a chain of Corner Houses which were known for quality, inexpensive catering. Some were quite large, offering food and music to over a thousand people. The waitresses were known for their speedy and polite service.

What had made shaving and the cleaning of teeth easier by the 1930s?

The safety razor and toothpaste (instead of powder)

Who set a new land-speed record in March, driving his car the Bluebird?

Sir Malcolm Campbell

The 47-year-old established a new record of 272 mph at Daytona Beach, Florida. The *Bluebird* was powered by an aircraft engine. During this record-breaking attempt, Campbell hit a bump on the 20-mile beach and travelled through the air for 30 feet. Sir Malcolm went on to establish several new land-speed records in the *Bluebird* and eventually died during another record-breaking attempt, in January 1949.

Who, in her film She Done Him Wrong, *asked Cary Grant to "Come up sometime, see me"?*

Mae West

This was the film version of West's stage hit, *Diamond Lil*. Mae West was too near the bone for 1930s Hollywood and much of the original show was toned down. (Even Diamond Lil was renamed Lady Lou.) Mae still managed to get her meanings across. The saloon-keeper she plays in the film describes herself as "one of the finest women who ever walked the streets". The film's songs included *I like a man who takes his time*. Later in 1933 West wrote and starred in *I'm No Angel*, where she played a circus performer. This is where she said, "It's not the men in my life but the life in my men." Both films were huge successes, as was *Klondike Annie* (1936).

Who ate spinach to give him strength?

Popeye

Popeye the Sailorman cartoons were first made by Paramount in 1933. Other characters included Olive Oyl (Popeye's girlfriend) and the bully Bluto. A total of 234 cinema Popeye cartoons were produced and in the 1950s the character was transferred to television and 200 more were made for the small screen.

Who played Tugboat Annie?

Marie Dressler

What did 250,000 people watch Queen Mary name on a rainy September day on Clydebank?

The liner, *Queen Mary*, as she launched it

This was the age of luxury ocean-going liners. The Cunard *Queen Mary* was designed as the largest, fastest liner ever built at the time. She was originally to have been launched in 1932 but work on the ship was stopped in 1931, as the economic depression worsened. Five thousand Clydeside shipyard workers had lost their jobs as a result. The ship's maiden voyage was made in May 1936, when she sailed from Southampton to New York. In August 1936 she regained the 'Blue Riband', awarded to the fastest liner across the Atlantic. The *Queen Mary's* crossing time was 3 days, 23 hours and 57 minutes.

Where in July did George V open a tunnel which carried traffic under a major river?

Liverpool (the Mersey Tunnel)

On 18 July the King's car was the first to enter the new tunnel. At the time it was the world's longest underwater tunnel. It had taken nearly nine years to dig and had cost almost seven million pounds.

Many large building and engineering projects were temporarily suspended during 1932/3 as the new National Government sought to limit public expenditure. The building of new schools and roads practically stopped for a period. The Mersey Tunnel was one of several major projects (such as the North Circular Road) which were begun in the 1920s.

What London landmark began to be demolished in June?

Waterloo Bridge

Designed by John Rennie and opened in 1817, Waterloo Bridge was regarded as the finest in London. Unfortunately its centre piers had begun to subside in 1923. A definite curve could be seen in the roadway. Further subsidence convinced engineers of the need for a new bridge, though this caused great controversy amongst admirers of the original. At the end of June, 700 of its granite balusters were offered to the public at £1 each and the two and a half hundredweight souvenirs were snapped up. In October, Sir Giles Scott's design for a new bridge was adopted by London County Council.

What were restrictions imposed on in London on 27 June?

The use of water (because of serious drought)

What sort of instrument did Reg Dixon play?

The organ

Dixon was the organist at the Tower Ballroom, Blackpool. In the 1930s he was a radio regular with his midday request programmes. Dixon's well-known signature tune was *I Do Like to Be Beside the Seaside*.

Who was the bad-tempered bird who made his screen debut in this year?

Donald Duck

Donald began his career as a co-star in *Mickey Mouse* short cartoons. In 1937 he was given his own series of shorts and regular cartoons were to be made until 1956. Various 'specials' were made after this and Donald and Mickey still appear frequently on television. Donald's most distinctive feature is his squawking voice, which was produced by the same man (Clarence Nash) from the first cartoon until 1969.

Who won his only Oscar opposite Claudette Colbert in It Happened One Night?

Clark Gable

One of Hollywood's biggest ever stars, Gable appeared in the box-office top ten from 1932 to 1943 and from 1947 to 1949. His many female co-stars included Joan Crawford (eight films) and Myrna Loy (seven films). Gable also received Oscar nominations for his part as Fletcher Christian in *Mutiny on the Bounty* (1935) and for his famous Rhett Butler in *Gone with the Wind* (1939). It was as Rhett Butler that he delivered his well-known line, "Frankly my dear, I don't give a damn."

Who was the song I Only Have Eyes For You *sung about in the movie* Dames?

Ruby Keeler

What road safety development was introduced by, and named after, Leslie Hore-Belisha?

The Belisha Beacon

Hore-Belisha was the Minister of Transport. In a bid to reduce injuries from road accidents, the government introduced a number of measures. These included road crossings for pedestrians, the first of which was set up in Central London. Crossings were marked at each end by a flashing yellow globe on a black and white post, known as a Belisha Beacon.

What was a Red Panther?

A motor-cycle

The 250cc Red Panther was a cheap model of motor-cycle introduced in 1932. The 1934 retail price was £29 17s 6d. The Panther was one of several cheap machines produced in a cost-cutting war as firms tried to win the restricted market caused by unemployment and short time.

Panthers were aimed at providing a ride-to-work machine for factory workers. They were most likely to be found garaged in back yards, covered by an old sack and fed the cheapest possible oil and fuel. However the machine did provide extraordinary value for money and remained on offer until just before the Second World War broke out. The motor-cycle was a very important feature of road transport in 1930s Britain. By 1937, one vehicle in every five was a two-wheeler.

What new form of gambling brought in £20 million during the football season in 1934/5?

The football pools

This was a new and inexpensive form of gambling which was to prove enormously popular with working people. It provided a cheap distraction for many people with little money to spare for entertainment. A jackpot win in the Penny Pool could be as large as £13,000 — a huge amount at the time.

Another outlet for gambling was provided by the growth of greyhound racing during the 1930s. Dog tracks appeared in several cities. As with association football, going to the dogs was an all-male pastime.

What became available to millions of schoolchildren at the end of the year for the price of one halfpenny per half-pint?

Milk (from a temporary period of surplus production)

Which Greek Princess married Prince George (the Duke of Kent) in November?

Princess Marina

In the two months before her marriage, Marina became a popular figure. She became a fashion leader, with her hats being especially noted and copies of them being produced. The Duke of Kent was the youngest of King George's three sons. After the wedding at Westminster Abbey, a Greek ceremony was held at Buckingham Palace.

Which 1930s movie star had originally been called Lucille Le Sueur, but was renamed by the winner of a magazine competition?

Joan Crawford

Crawford had worked her way up through small parts, having been a chorus girl and understudy in the late 1920s. Her career was at its height in the mid-1930s, when she was frequently teamed with Clark Gable (*Dancing Lady*, 1933; *Chained*, 1934). Her career began to slide at the end of the decade and she left MGM to do war work during the US war years.

She made an acting comeback in *Mildred Pierce* (1945) for which she won an Oscar. This was followed by *Humoresque* (1946) and then a number of poor films (including *Flamingo Road*, 1949 and *Johnny Guitar*, 1954) which led to another retirement, during which she concentrated on a new career as a business associate of her fourth husband, who was chairman of Pepsi Cola. In 1962 she made another successful comeback with *Whatever Happened to Baby Jane?* in which Crawford and Bette Davis played sisters, both Hollywood 'has-beens'.

Who sang his trademark song, Inka Dinka Doo, *in the film* Palooka?

Jimmy Durante

Durante was the comedian/singer/actor with a big nose, gravelly voice and mangled English. During the 1930s he was a stage performer, appearing in Broadway shows such as *Strike me Pink* and *Jumbo*. He had his first starring film role in *Palooka*, alongside Jimmy Cagney's brother, William. During the 1940s he made more film appearances, including *Music for Millions* (1944) and *This Time for Keeps* (1947). *The Milkman* (1950) included the song, *That's My Boy*.

Which Englishman became the Wimbledon singles champion this year?

Fred Perry

What opened at Leicester Square in May and had the world's longest escalator?

Leicester Square tube station

The tube had been gradually extended from the early years of the century. In 1926 the 17-mile extension to the Northern line had been the world's longest tunnel. Piccadilly Circus Underground Station had opened in 1928. The tube had already seen strikes (1924) and fatal accidents (1938). During the Blitz, underground stations were used by some as shelters. The government did not encourage this as stations became overcrowded and insanitary. Relatively few Londoners sheltered in the tube, most spending air raids at home in their own shelters.

Which Hollywood cowboy and film comedian was killed in an aircrash in August?

Will Rogers

Rogers crashed in Northern Alaska while on a flight attempt across the North Pole to Moscow. He had been making this journey with Wiley Post, a well-known American airman. The one-eyed Post had been the first man to fly solo around the world, in 1933. The wise-cracking cowboy and Post were found in the wreckage of the Americans pilot's *Flying Bird* aeroplane.

Who replaced Ramsay MacDonald as Prime Minister of the National Government in June?

Stanley Baldwin

MacDonald resigned as Prime Minister through ill-health. Technically he swapped places with his number two, Stanley Baldwin. In reality MacDonald's political career was effectively over. He was even to lose his seat in the 1935 General Election. Baldwin had been Prime Minister of Conservative administrations twice before — the National Government was now Conservative in all but name (even more so after the 1935 election). The 1935 election saw the National Government returned with a huge majority. Of its successful candidates, 432 were Tories and 20 Liberals. The opposition was made up of 154 Labour MPs.

Which African country did Mussolini's Italian troops invade in October?

Abyssinia

Who was the handsome, swashbuckling hero who became a star in the pirate tale, Captain Blood?

Errol Flynn

Flynn established himself in a series of classic, historical adventure pictures in the 1930s. *Captain Blood* was followed by *The Charge of the Light Brigade* (1936) and *The Adventures of Robin Hood* (1938). Flynn made over 50 films in his career. In the 1940s these included *They Died with Their Boots On* (1941) and *Objective Burma* (1945).

Whose catchphrase was "Can you hear me, mother?"?

Sandy Powell

Powell was a roly-poly, north-country comedian. His catchphrase was derived from his nervous first appearance on the radio. As with many 1930s comedians, Powell could be seen live in local variety theatres and heard on the radio. Comic monologues such as 'Sandy Powell at the zoo' could also be heard on gramophone records. Some of the better comedians appeared in feature films. Others had to content themselves with performing for a section of the weekly 10-minute magazine called *Pathe Pictorial*. Powell managed to appear in several rather poor low-budget films.

What made this year's movie, Becky Sharp, *stand out?*

It was the first, full-length, colour feature film

The new three-colour Technicolor process had already been used in a few short films and for segments at the end of three films in 1934. It had never before been used in an entire feature film. Cinemagoers were attracted to *Becky Sharp* by the new technique. The film itself was unfortunately rather dull and did not feature any big-name attractions.

To many, the new Technicolor was lurid, especially in showing actors' complexions. Some actresses refused to be photographed in it. This early form of Technicolor used three individual negatives sensitive to red, blue and green. A major drawback was its cost. There was not a big rush to adopt the new technique (there were still only 28 colour features in Hollywood by 1945). Only when cheaper and more realistic processes became available, such as Eastmancolor in the early 1950s, was the use of colour to begin to grow.

Who grew a moustache for his starring role in this year's movie, The Lives of a Bengal Lancer?

Gary Cooper

What first appeared in the middle of British roads in this year?

Cats' eyes

The installation of these glass reflectors was only one of the safety measures being introduced to reduce the dangers of motoring. The 30 mph speed limit for built-up areas was imposed in March of the same year. Compulsory dipped car headlights were announced in July. The newly controlled motorists were having to pay 1/6d per gallon for their petrol.

What did drivers now have to do for the first time?

Pass a driving test

Early motorists had become notorious for their dangerous driving. Lessons were taken anyhow, from fathers or friends, and nobody had to pass any kind of test. Even the new test was not applied to drivers who already had a licence. It would be several years before the majority of motorists had passed their driving tests.

What was completed in 1935, bringing electricity to almost all areas of the country?

The National Grid

The electricity supply industry increased its number of consumers from three quarters of a million in 1920 to nine million in 1939. Its first use in the home had been to replace gas lighting, but its growth during the 1930s also enabled and encouraged a growth in the use of electrical appliances. Only a very small minority used it for cooking and heating. Refrigerators were also rare. The number of irons and vacuum cleaners was increasing more rapidly. (Production of vacuum cleaners increased dramatically between 1930 and 1935, from 37,550 to 409,345.) Many of the new electrical devices were rather crude, as was domestic wiring in a lot of cases.

What new type of book began to appear on newsagents' shelves in orange and white covers, priced sixpence?

Penguin paperbacks (*Ariel* and *A Farewell to Arms* were the first)

What sort of musician was Geraldo?

A popular dance band leader

Geraldo starred in several pre-Second World War radio series. These included *Dancing Through* in 1934 and *Romance in Rhythm* in 1935. He also enjoyed broadcasting success during the Second World War. His signature tune was *Hello Again, We're on the Radio Again*. The 1930s were a great period for dance band music. Bands were identified by their leaders. The vocalists on hit records were often not even named. Other popular band leaders included Jack Hylton, Roy Fox and Ambrose.

Who scored seven goals for Arsenal against Aston Villa in December?

Ted Drake

Arsenal were the most successful football team during the 1930s. They won the League five times in the decade and the FA Cup twice. Drake was one of Arsenal's many England internationals. No less than seven Arsenal players, including Wilf Copping and Eddie Hapgood, appeared for the same England team in the 1934 defeat of Italy (3–2). Arsenal's reputation was established in the early years of the decade, under manager Herbert Chapman, who died in 1934. The team was also involved in the biggest upset of the decade, being beaten 2–0 in the FA Cup by Third Division Walsall in 1933.

In May, Mr T E Shaw died in a motorcycle accident in Dorset. As whom is he better remembered?

Colonel T E Lawrence (Lawrence of Arabia)

Lawrence was famous for his First World War exploits, when he led an Arab rebellion against the Turks. He is also remembered as a literary figure, though he would not allow his best-known work, *The Seven Pillars of Wisdom*, to be published during his lifetime. Lawrence was an eccentric figure. After the First World War he was to spend 14 years in the RAF as an ordinary aircraftsman, under the name of Shaw. He had only left the RAF two months before his fatal road accident.

Who stood trial with her 19-year-old chauffeur, George Stoner, for the murder of her 67-year-old husband in a celebrated trial in June?

Mrs Rattenbury

Who did George McMahon threaten with a revolver on 16 July?

The King (Edward VIII)

The King was returning along Constitution Hill to Buckingham Palace. He was at the head of six battalions of Guards to whom he had presented new colours in Hyde Park. As the King drew near, McMahon produced a revolver. A policeman managed to seize him and knock the revolver away. The gun fell into the road and McMahon (described as a Scottish journalist) was dragged away. He was charged with being in possession of a revolver with intent to endanger life (the gun had been loaded). In September the somewhat unstable McMahon was given 12 months' hard labour.

Who did the King (Edward VIII) abdicate to marry?

Mrs Wallace Simpson

Mrs Simpson was married, already divorced once, 39-years-old and American. She was possibly the least suitable match for the King of England that could be imagined. At first, Edward's association with her was given a low profile in British newspapers, but eventually he was being publicly criticized in Britain and the story was widely featured in the British Press.

Mrs Simpson was given her second divorce in October 1936. The King made his intention to marry her known by November. This led to a crisis. The Church opposed the marriage because Mrs Simpson was a divorcee. A suggested compromise, whereby Edward could marry Mrs Simpson without her becoming Queen, was rejected. It became clear that the King faced a simple choice between the throne and Mrs Simpson. Edward chose the latter and abdicated on 10 December 1936. He was succeeded by his brother, Albert, the Duke of York, who became George VI. Edward broadcast the reasons for his decision on the radio the following day, before going into exile as the Duke of Windsor.

Which famous London landmark was burnt to the ground on 30 November?

The Crystal Palace

The Palace had originally been built for the Great Exhibition of 1851. It had become one of London's most familiar sights. The blaze which destroyed the Palace could be seen from nearly 80 miles away. Thousands of Londoners travelled across the city to watch the fire and the unsuccessful attempts to control it.

What set out from the North-eastern town of Jarrow on 5 October?

The Jarrow Crusade

Who sang When I'm Cleaning Windows *as he stood on a ladder in the film,* Keep Your Seats Please*?*

George Formby

This toothy, ukelele-playing Northerner packed in British cinema audiences in the late 1930s and early 1940s. He was well known for his broad grin, strong Lancashire accent and simple, catchy songs, such as *Leaning on a Lamp-Post*. Formby's films were low-budget, British productions which included *It's in the Air* (1938) and *Come On, George* (1939). One film used a Formby catchphrase as its title — *Turned Out Nice Again* (1941).

Which movie featured three big stars and an earthquake?

San Francisco

MGM brought in three big names for this picture: Clark Gable, Jeanette MacDonald and Spencer Tracy. However the biggest star of the film was the 10-minute long, skilfully developed sequence which showed the destruction of San Francisco in April 1906. This was the most impressive piece of special-effects work since *King Kong*. It used 400 extras and was the work of several artists. MGM's efforts were worthwhile as *San Francisco* was their biggest profit-maker of the decade, taking $2,237,000 on its first five years' release world-wide.

Which elderly washer woman made her film debut in this year?

Old Mother Riley

This was in reality a man — Arthur Lucan. He originally played this comedy character in a stage act with his wife, Kitty McShane. Mother Riley went on to appear in 14 British films. Their titles all began with *Old Mother Riley . . .*, as in *Old Mother Riley Joins Up* (1940). The films all followed a similar type of storyline and featured McShane as Mother Riley's daughter Kitty. Lucan had a troubled marriage with McShane which eventually broke up. He was dominated by his forceful wife and suffered illness and drink problems.

What sport, established in Britain over the 1930s, attracted 75,000 to Wembley for its first World Individual Riders Championship Final?

Speedway

What did the electric, self-heating irons now available often plug into?

A light socket

Electricity was still only recently available to many. Often homes did not have sockets for domestic appliances. Irons could be plugged into a light socket with a two-way adaptor. This enabled people to iron and still have the light on.

What did Mr Drage promise to deliver in a plain van?

Furniture bought on hire-purchase

HP or the never-never was an innovation of the 1930s. It enabled householders without capital to purchase some of the growing range of domestic equipment (electric irons, radios, fires etc). It also gave an increasing number of better-off people the opportunity to obtain one of the growing number of private motor-cars. Attitudes to hire-purchase were very different from those of today. The never-never was still not quite respectable to many. This explains the leading hire-purchase firms' guarantee to deliver their furniture in plain vans.

What famous voice began to tell the time on 24 July?

The Speaking Clock

In 1935, a Croydon telephonist had won a GPO competition to find the voice for this new service. In its first week 248,828 calls were made to it.

What was the new word game which was now popular?

Lexicon

Who received 130,000 cards on her eighth birthday?

Shirley Temple

This little girl was a tremendously popular movie star during the 1930s. Her films included *Little Miss Marker* (1934), *Curly Top* (1935), *Dimples* (1936) and *Wee Willie Winkie* (1937). She made 42 movies in all and is often remembered singing the song *On the Good Ship Lollipop*.

Escapism was the order of the day in 1930s cinema and this resulted in two of its biggest box-office attractions being a small girl and an Alsatian (Rin Tin Tin).

Which American athlete won four gold medals at the Berlin Olympics and proved a great embarrassment to Adolf Hitler?

Jesse Owens

The Nazis tried to use the Berlin Games to impress the world. The Berlin Olympics were both spectacular and efficiently organized. One of Hitler's central beliefs was the idea of a superior race. People such as Jews and Negroes were regarded as inferior to Aryans (white, Germanic types). It was unfortunate for Hitler that the undisputed star of the Berlin Games was the American Negro runner Jesse Owens. The black athlete's four victories (100 metres, 200 metres, long jump and 4 × 100 metres relay) were not a good advert for Nazi beliefs and Hitler refused to congratulate Owens on any of his golds.

Who starred with Jeanette MacDonald in the film Rose Marie*?*

Nelson Eddy

MacDonald and Eddy are often remembered as a couple in screen romances. They appeared together in nine musicals between 1935 and 1942. Their first film together was *Naughty Marietta* (1935) which included the songs *Ah! Sweet Mystery of Life* and *Italian Street Song*. *Rose Marie* was their next film. In it, Eddy played a Canadian Mountie. It was this film which featured the songs *Indian Love Call* and *Rose Marie*.

Who was the short, paunchy Governor of the Canary Isles who led rebel Spanish troops from Morocco into Southern Spain to fight in the Civil War?

General Franco

What did 10 million people throng to London to see on 12 May?

The Coronation of George VI

40,000 servicemen lined the route to Westminster Abbey taken by the six-mile long procession. The crowds were packed along the way taken by the carriages and bands. Unfortunately London's 260,000 busmen had been on strike since 1 May. This meant that the coronation crowds had to walk into the city. Luckily the weather was fine for the day. The crowning itself was performed by Dr Cosmo Gordon Lang, the 72-year-old Archbishop of Canterbury. That night the newly-crowned George VI broadcast to the Empire.

What was the name of Britain's first aircraft carrier, launched on 20 April at Birkenhead?

HMS *Ark Royal*

Britain had begun to rearm in the face of the growing threat from Germany. Increasing amounts of the money spent were to be directed to the newer areas of warfare. (Money spent on the RAF rose from £17 million in 1935 to £133 million in 1939.) £3 million of the navy's money was spent on building their first aircraft carrier. The *Ark Royal* was to see much action in the early years of the Second World War. The carrier's aircraft accounted for the loss of much enemy shipping and over 100 enemy planes. On 13 November 1941 she was torpedoed and sunk in the Mediterranean by a U-boat.

What was the name of the giant German airship which exploded in America in May?

The *Hindenburg*

The Germans had pioneered the use of the airship. Even accidents such as those of the R101 and the American Akron (1933) had not ended German enthusiasm for this form of flight. Previous to its New Jersey crash, the *Hindenburg* had made 10 two-way crossings of the Atlantic, each perfectly safely. However after the *Hindenburg* disaster all further flights by hydrogen-filled airships were banned — by Adolf Hitler.

Who was the Chancellor of the Exchequer who succeeded Stanley Baldwin as Prime Minister in May?

Neville Chamberlain

What is the second line of the song Underneath the Arches?

'We dream our dreams away'

This famous song was performed by Bud Flanagan and Chesney Allen. They were popular variety performers who worked together as part of the Crazy Gang. The Gang had six members (in three double acts): Jimmy Nervo and Teddy Knox, Charlie Naughton and Jimmy Gold, Bud Flanagan and Chesney Allen. The Gang featured in several films, including *Alf's Button Afloat* (1938) and *Gasbags* (1940). Flanagan and Allen were always the Gang's best known members. Chesney Allen was the well-dressed straight man and Bud Flanagan the more directly funny. They made a film entitled *Underneath the Arches* in 1937.

Who was the teenage girl with a soprano voice who starred in One Hundred Men and a Girl?

Deanna Durbin

Durbin was a popular young talent of the late 1930s. Her cheery musicals featured semi-operatic versions of popular songs such as *Moonlight Bay* and *Someone to Care for Me*. She made 21 musicals between 1936 and 1947. These included *Three Smart Girls* (1936), *Mad About Music* (1938) and *That Certain Age* (1938). The plots of these films were very predictable, with Durbin always playing a perky heroine who makes everything come to a happy conclusion. As with the work of Shirley Temple, Durbin's escapist films became less popular as she grew older. Her movies were still well-liked in the early 1940s, but once Durbin entered her twenties her audience began to diminish rapidly.

What very popular song did Lupino Lane sing in the stage show Me and My Girl? *(It also came to accompany a well-known dance.)*

The Lambeth Walk

The stage-show *Me and My Girl* was on the verge of closing down when the BBC broadcast some excerpts from it on the radio. The attention that this brought the ailing show helped turn it into a great success. A dance was invented to suit the song. This involved a swagger, thumbs-up and "Oi". The song itself sold more copies than any since *Yes, We Have No Bananas*. The opening lines of the song were:

'Any time you're Lambeth way,
Any evening, any day,
You'll find us all doin' the Lambeth Walk.'

Who were Harpo, Zeppo, Chico and Groucho?

The Marx Brothers

What did Billy Butlin first set up in Skegness?

A commercial holiday camp

Two years later, holiday camps had accommodation for half a million. The camps offered all-in holidays based on chalets and providing modern catering and leisure facilities. They were a great improvement on the seaside boarding house holidays taken by many working people.

What well-known children's comic introduced Dennis the Menace in 1937?

The *Dandy*

An innovation in children's reading in the 1930s was the development of coloured comics. The *Dandy* was launched in 1937 and the *Beano* in 1938. These were to introduce Desperate Dan and Biffo the Bear. The newer coloured comics competed with and replaced the more old-fashioned two-colour *Magnet* and *Gem*. Schoolboy reading included other colour comics such as the *Hotspur* and *Wizard*.

What well-known telephone number began to connect callers with Scotland Yard from 29 November?

999

The introduction of the emergency number was one of several innovations made by the police force at this time. Another new development was the first use of dogs by Scotland Yard, in 1938. The introduction of new traffic regulations pointed the way in which the force would grow. Speed limits inevitably led to the growth in numbers of traffic police to enforce them. For the moment a small number of police cars fitted with bells patrolled the roads. In the age before mass car ownership, these new services were a very small part of the force, which depended almost entirely upon the efforts of the bobby on the beat. The lack of large-scale car-related crime made the job of policing a very different task.

What did you join when you wrote to 42 Upper Grosvenor Street, London W1 for your badge, official rule book and secret code book?

The League of Ovaltineys

Who was the ex-vicar killed by a lion this year?

Harold Davidson (ex-Rector of Stiffkey)

In 1932 Davidson had provided the popular Sunday newspapers with one of the most sensational stories that they covered during the 1930s. At the time, Davidson was the Rector of Stiffkey, a small parish in Norfolk. Unfortunately his pastoral work was mainly with chorus girls and waitresses. In 1932 he had been brought before a Church court who unfrocked him and found him guilty of causing 'grave scandal to the Church'. The stories of Davidson setting up young women in his London lodgings were followed keenly by the newspapers' readers.

After the revelation of his activities, Davidson took a number of disreputable jobs. In 1937 he was earning money by exhibiting himself with the lions in a circus. He made the news again after he had been badly mauled by a lion and died of his injuries. The incident happened at a Skegness funfair and the lion's name was Freddie.

Who set out from Miami, Florida on 1 June to make a round-the-world flight?

Amelia Earhart

Having visited South America, Africa, India and Batavia her plane (a £20,000 Lockheed Electra) was lost on the final stages of her journey in mid-Pacific. She was never seen again and, after intensive search, was presumed dead. The American 'Lady Lindy' Earhart was the first woman to fly the Atlantic solo (in 1928).

Who was the brave Welshman narrowly defeated by Joe Louis in the American's first defence of the world heavyweight boxing title?

Tommy Farr

Farr's long career had begun in the travelling boxing-booths. Not a powerful puncher, he developed a curious crouching and weaving style. The British title-holder got his big chance when he was nominated as first challenger to the new world champion. No Briton had fought for the heavyweight crown for nearly 30 years. Boxing fans throughout the UK got up in the early hours to hear the radio commentary on the title bout, staged in New York on 30 August. Farr fought fiercely early on but Louis fought back for a narrow points win. The Welshman's boxing career was halted by the war. In 1950, aged 36 and after 10 years out of the ring, Farr made an astonishing comeback. In three years he fought his way to a final eliminator for the British title, but lost.

Who went from Shangri-La (in Lost Horizon*) to Ruritania (in* The Prisoner of Zenda*)?*

Ronald Colman

Britain's highest-paid film and stage star became a CBE (Commander of the Order of the British Empire) in this year. Who was she?

Gracie Fields

The Lancashire Lass became hugely popular with songs such as *Sally* and comic lyrics including 'Walter, Lead Me to the Altar'. She also made a number of films in the 1930s, including *Sally in our Alley* (1931) and *Shipyard Sally* (1939) — this featured the first big hit song of the war, *Wish Me Luck As You Wave Me Goodbye*. The title of this song was to prove ironic as Fields left Britain for the duration of the war when all Italians were interned as enemy aliens. This was a result of her having married an Italian, her producer Monty Banks. 'Our Gracie' was to go through a period of public disapproval when she left for Hollywood with her husband, as Italy declared war.

Where did Neville Chamberlain fly to on 29 September?

Munich

Hitler's territorial ambitions had recently focused on the Sudetenland area of Czechoslovakia, which had a large, ethnically German population. Public opinion in Britain, at first, had not been greatly aroused by a quarrel in Eastern Europe over a place few people had ever heard of. This indifference turned to a degree of apprehension after the fleet had been mobilized and a few primitive anti-aircraft precautions were made in London. At a four-power conference on 29 September Hitler's demands were accepted and the Czechs were told that they must accept the agreement. The Sudetenland was occupied by the Germans and the sovereignty of the rest of Czechoslovakia was guaranteed by the four powers. It was this agreement which Chamberlain described as 'peace for our time'. All the press and most ordinary people were glad that war had been avoided and supported the agreement. In March 1939, Hitler's troops occupied the rest of Czechoslovakia.

Who was the American tycoon who set a new record for round-the-world flight in July?

Howard Hughes

The millionaire film producer and four companions flew their 14-seater Lockheed airliner nearly 15,000 miles round the world in 91 hours. They flew via Paris, Moscow, Omsk, Alaska and Minneapolis. Hughes and his crew cut the previous record for round-the-world flight in half. They received a ticker-tape welcome when they returned to New York. Howard Hughes was later to become known for his existence as a millionaire recluse.

Which streamlined British locomotive set a new world speed record for steam engines of 126 mph on 3 July?

The Mallard

Which famous film partnership danced to the song Change Partners *in the movie* Carefree?

Fred Astaire and Ginger Rogers

First brought together in a film of their own in 1933, Astaire and Rogers made a succession of musicals in the 1930s. Dance routines to songs such as *Lovely to Look at*, in *Roberta* (1935), *Cheek to Cheek*, in *Top Hat* (1935) and *Let's Call the Whole Thing Off*, in *Shall We Dance?* (1937) made their films big box-office successes. The partnership broke up in 1939. The Astaire/Rogers movies featured scores by Cole Porter, Jerome Kern, the Gershwins and Irving Berlin.

Name the seven dwarfs in Walt Disney's Snow White and the Seven Dwarfs.

Happy, Sleepy, Bashful, Sneezy, Grumpy, Dopey and Doc

This was Disney's first feature-length cartoon. Previously his work had been in short films with characters such as Mickey Mouse and Donald Duck. The seven dwarfs are well-known for their choruses, *Whistle While You Work* and *Hi-Ho Hi-Ho, It's Off to Work We Go.* The film's sentimental story is summed up in Snow White's own song, *Some Day My Prince Will Come*. Snow White's Prince wakes her from a death-like sleep with a kiss.

Which radio comedy series did Arthur Askey star in with Richard Murdoch?

Bandwagon

Big-Hearted Arthur was a Cockney comic whose catchphrase in this show was "Aythankiow". *Bandwagon* featured Askey and Murdoch in an imaginary flat above Broadcasting House. The war broke this partnership up, though both went on to do a range of radio work: Murdoch wrote and starred in *Much Binding in the Marsh* and Askey had his own radio show.

Which of this year's movies concerned a fictional band that featured Tyrone Power as bandleader, Alice Faye as singer and Don Ameche on piano?

Alexander's Ragtime Band

How much did the new magazine Picture Post cost when it was launched this year?

Thruppence (3d)

Several new popular magazines were launched in the 1930s. Some, like *Picture Post*, are no longer produced. Others, like *Woman*, which was launched in 1937, priced 2d, are still with us. *Picture Post* made abundant use of photographs to illustrate articles on current events and features on other subjects.

What was Bakelite?

Bakelite was one of the new plastics being produced

Bakelite's chief use was as a substitute for materials such as wood and bone, since it did not warp or rot. Plastics could be moulded into any shape and this did away with any need for the turning, planing or finishing necessary with wood. They could also be coloured in the making.

One of the most noticeable effects of the increase in the use of plastics was that it made many items affordable for many more people. Radios began to be mass-produced in plastic casings and became available at a much cheaper price. Earlier in the decade, radios had still been expensive items, usually in veneered wood casings. A Marconi radio in veneered casing was available at eleven and a half guineas. Mass-production in Bakelite made radios available to almost every household. The great age of mass radio listening was reaching its peak. Not only had access to radio sets grown, but there was, as yet, almost no competition from television.

What did the police recommend should be fitted with a rear light in April this year?

All bicycles

The bicycle was a very important form of transport when only a small proportion of people owned cars. It provided a cheap way of getting to and from work. Cycling was also a popular leisure pastime. It enabled many to get out into the country or even to take an inexpensive cycling holiday. In 1935 the Road Traffic Census had shown a 95 per cent increase in the number of bicycles on the road over the previous four years.

What was supplied detached from men's shirts?

The collar

Who was the Cheeky Chappie?

Max Miller

Miller was a popular Cockney comedian. His stage act was considered 'saucy' at the time and got him into trouble on the radio. Typical was his story of looking for lodgings and asking the landlady if she could squeeze him in the back room. Max's signature tune was *Mary from the Dairy*, to which he would stride on stage in one of his silk floral suits. His rapid patter included the catch-phrase, "There'll never be another, will there lady?" Miller appeared in several, rather poor films in the late 1930s (among them *Transatlantic Trouble*, 1937 and *Thank Evans*, 1938).

Who was the super-hero who thrilled children in Saturday matinees as he fought against Ming the Merciless?

Flash Gordon

Flash was the hero in three serials (around 15-parts long) made for the cinema. Originally an American comic-strip hero, Flash, with his friends, fought the evil Ming to secure the Earth's safety. The three serials made were *Flash Gordon* (1936), *Flash Gordon's Trip to Mars* (1938) and *Flash Gordon Conquers the Universe* (1940). The hero was played by Buster Crabbe, a former Olympic swimmer, who also featured in many B westerns as Buck Rogers, another serial hero.

Which young Yorkshire batsman scored a record innings of 364 runs for England in the final Test Match at the Oval?

Len Hutton

England's cricketers managed to defeat the Australians by the unprecedented margin of an innings and 579 runs to level this series. Much of this was due to Hutton's incredible innings, which lasted a full 13 hours 17 minutes. He exceeded Don Bradman's previous test record by 30 runs.

Len Hutton's long career had many highlights. On 16 July 1951 he scored his one hundredth century. Hutton became the first professional cricketer to captain England in June 1953. In the 1956 Birthday Honours list he was knighted for his service to the game.

Who was Father Flanagan in Boys' Town?

Spencer Tracy

What was introduced for young men on 26 April?

Conscription

British preparations for the eventuality of war were now being taken more seriously. The armed forces were being increased in size, with the government introducing conscription for young men of 20–21. The first conscripts were enrolled on 3 June. A conscript received his enlistment notice through the post, together with a travel warrant and a few shillings advance pay. He then had a few days to settle his affairs, notify his employer and report to a stated forces training centre for service.

Where were five people killed by an IRA bomb on 25 August?

Coventry

This was the worst explosion since the IRA had begun this latest bombing campaign at the start of the year. The bomb was planted in a tradesman's box-tricycle left standing in Broadgate, the main street of Coventry centre. The bomb exploded just before 2.30 pm, shattering 25 shopfronts and injuring 50 people. Other targets for IRA attacks made in 1939 included Piccadilly Circus, Victoria and Kings Cross stations, Manchester and Birmingham.

What did Britain do at 11.00 am on 3 September?

It declared war on Germany

Since the Czechoslovakian collapse, Britain had been searching for allies who they felt would strengthen their position against Germany. This had led them into an alliance with Poland, which involved giving the Poles an assurance that Britain and France would support them should their independence be threatened. On 31 August, Hitler gave the order to attack Poland. At 4.45 am on 1 September, German troops crossed the Polish frontier. The Poles appealed to their ally, which was hesitant. Attempts were made to find a solution without declaring war. Even after the Cabinet had voted to send an ultimatum to Germany, those opposed to such direct action were trying to negotiate a conference for the withdrawal of German troops. The strength of opinion behind taking a strong line became more evident. The ultimatum was delivered to the German government at 9.00 am on 3 September. This asked that Germany should halt its attack on Poland. When the Germans made no reply before the ultimatum's expiry at 11.00 am, a state of war was entered into.

What was the German pocket-battleship which was scuttled in the river Plate, off Montevideo, after being attacked by the cruisers Exeter, Ajax *and* Achilles?

The *Admiral Graf Spee*

Which famous detective did Basil Rathbone play in a series of films which began in 1939?

Sherlock Holmes

Holmes has been played by many actors, but Rathbone is the actor most often associated with the Victorian sleuth. Rathbone's Holmes films were not classics. They were mostly B movies, about one hour long. Nigel Bruce played Holmes's companion, Dr Watson. The series began with *The Hound of the Baskervilles* (1939) and ended (after 14 films) with *Dressed to Kill* (1946). Rathbone was also a notable villain in films such as *The Adventures of Robin Hood* (1938) and *The Mark of Zorro* (1940).

Which British actor won an Oscar for his role as the schoolteacher Mr Chips?

Robert Donat

In *Goodbye Mr Chips*, Donat played a master at an English public school. The film also starred Greer Garson as his wife. By winning the Oscar for best actor in this year, Donat had beaten Clark Gable, who had been nominated for his role as Rhett Butler in *Gone With The Wind*. Donat had also received an Oscar nomination in 1938 for his role as a young Welsh doctor in *The Citadel*. These two films were the high points of Donat's career, which was hampered by ill health (chronic asthma).

In which film did Judy Garland (as the young girl, Dorothy) sing Over the Rainbow?

The Wizard of Oz

This film established the 16-year-old Garland as a major star. The movie was a fantasy musical adapted from a series of children's books. Other well-known characters included The Tin Man (who had no heart), The Scarecrow and Toto (Dorothy's dog). MGM spent $2 million producing this film which was amongst the earlier major colour films to be produced.

During the 1930s, the teenage Garland had been teamed with the young Mickey Rooney for a number of films, including three of the Andy Hardy series (among them *Love Finds Andy Hardy*, 1938).

What sort of instrument did Charlie Kunz play?

The piano

What was in the cardboard box now supposed to be carried by everyone?

A gas mask

The possible use of poison gas was a real fear before the war. Everybody was issued with a mask which was carried in a small cardboard box. People were told to put on their gas masks if they heard the gas rattles sound. Fortunately gas was never to be used in air-raids and the call to carry masks at all times was largely forgotten by 1940.

The heavy make-up worn by women at the time proved troublesome, as the heat inside the masks made mascara run. Elaborate hairstyles or heavy beards made fitting a mask difficult. Masks smelt strongly of disinfectant and rubber. People learnt to spit on the inside of the mica window in order to stop it misting up.

What happened to 827,000 schoolchildren in September?

They were evacuated

The government encouraged mothers to send children out of cities and into reception areas, away from the expected air-raids. Once in a safe area, evacuees were billeted with local people. Each child had an officially printed and franked postcard which they sent to their parents on arrival, with details of their new address.

Some 524,000 children under school age and their mothers, as well as 12,000 expectant mothers, also went out of the cities. Many of these evacuees went home after only a short period away. The lack of air-raids (after October 1939), homesickness and the imposition of a small (six shillings a week) parental contribution towards the support of evacuated children encouraged the drift back. The fall of France in June 1940 and the start of air attacks in the Autumn produced another substantial round of evacuation.

What unusual colour was much wartime petrol?

Red

Petrol for commercial vehicles was dyed red to stop it being used illicitly by civilians. There was still a good deal of petrol fiddling. Red petrol could be strained through a gas mask filter to remove the colour. Black market petrol could be had for 6/6d per gallon. Petrol rationing had begun on 16 September 1939, when branded petrol was replaced by pool, a medium octane blend (1/6d a gallon in September 1939).

What did the BBC National Service and Regional Service become on 1 September?

The BBC Home Service

PEOPLE

What sort of column did R H Naylor write for the Sunday Express?

The horoscopes

Towards the end of the 1930s, nearly all the popular newspapers were publishing horoscopes. Naylor was one of the best-known newspaper astrologers. His column featured a photograph of himself, which showed a middle-aged, bespectacled man lighting his pipe. In competition, another Sunday newspaper claimed to have obtained the services of the gypsy, Petulengro, to compile its horoscopes.

As which cowboy hero was William Boyd better known?

Hopalong Cassidy

This cowboy character was the hero of 66 Hollywood B films during the 1930s and 1940s. He was a very familiar figure to cinema audiences, dressed in an all-black outfit and riding his horse Topper. Hopalong later featured in his own television series in the 1950s and a Radio Luxembourg serial from 1953.

Who played Scarlett O'Hara in Gone With The Wind?

Vivien Leigh

The role of Scarlett O'Hara was one of the most sought-after in Hollywood. It was therefore surprising that an English actress with only a few films to her credit was chosen to play the Southern heroine. She had to have diction coaching in order to adjust her precise English delivery to the Dixieland tones of Scarlett. Leigh constantly battled with the film's director during the making of the movie. Despite this, she won an Oscar for her portrayal. Her films after *Gone With The Wind* included *Lady Hamilton* (1941), *Caesar and Cleopatra* (1945) and she was Blanche DuBois in *A Streetcar Named Desire* (1951).

Which young film actor got his first substantial part as the Ringo Kid in the cheaply made Western, Stagecoach?

John Wayne

the 1940s

THE **1940s** were dominated by the Second World War, which brought enormous changes to the everyday lives and surroundings of the British people. Unlike previous wars, it also exposed the civilian population to death and destruction through the German air-raids on British towns and cities.

The enormous reduction in imports and the need to supply a large fighting force produced massive shortages and rationing. Queuing became a way of life, while the black market opened opportunities to a less scrupulous minority. The call for increased factory production came at a time when millions of men were away in the services. Other workers had to take their place. Many women now found themselves in a variety of workplaces previously occupied mainly by men. These included factories, transport and the land. Women's broader experience of work is an example of the way the war led to a widening of people's outlooks, as compared with their more restricted peacetime lives.

The world-wide nature of the war led to many men being posted to places as varied as Egypt, Italy, France and Burma. This was at a time when very few British people had experience of foreign travel. The availability of cheap package holidays abroad was over 20 years away. At the same time, we should guard against accounts of battles in foreign countries giving us a false impression of servicemen's experience of the war. Most of a soldier's time was not spent fighting. Long periods were occupied by travelling, 'square bashing' and sitting in camp canteens, often in towns as exciting as Aldershot and Stafford! A common problem for many new recruits was the boredom of much service life.

Not only were many British soldiers sent to other parts of the world, but servicemen from other countries came to Britain. The Commonwealth countries of Canada, Australia and New Zealand were well represented. Refugees and troops from defeated continental allies, such as Poland, France and Norway, came to Britain early on in the war. These foreign soldiers provided an experience of other nationalities not usually gained in British towns. Later, when the United States entered the war, the Americans began to arrive. Interestingly, the GIs brought many British men and women their first contact with black people.

Ironically, at the same time as it gave many people a broader experience of life, the war also produced more restrictions than any other period of the century. An individual's movements and behaviour were subject to a barrage of official controls. People were told what they could buy, where they could go, when to turn their lights on and how deep their bathwater should be. Many of these regulations were not obeyed whole-heartedly. After an initial panic, the compulsory carrying of gas-masks began to be ignored. Many of the more petty regulations could never be properly enforced and were really a plea for self-control. Frequently people did not object to controls; more often they complained because they felt that the rules were not being applied equally.

The war brought tragedy to many families and destruction to people's homes. A total of 450,000 British servicemen were killed in six years' fighting and 60,000 civilians died in air attacks. These deaths meant that the victory celebrations of VE and VJ day were also sombre moments for a significant number of families. The war would never end for families left without a father or son. This means that great care needs to be taken when talking about the war. Careful listening can often detect possible distress before any upsetting incident occurs. People will often reveal distressing memories if they feel confident of a sensitive response. If possible, familiarize yourself with any known wartime deaths suffered by a person's family.

Despite the war's enormous importance, we must remember that the second half of the 1940s were lived in peace. However, although the actual fighting had ended in 1945, the war continued to influence people's lives and attitudes. Many of peacetime's biggest problems were direct results of the upheaval caused by the war. For every British civilian killed, 35 had been made homeless. Three and a half million houses had been damaged or destroyed in enemy air-raids. The subsequent housing shortage was one of the biggest difficulties facing Britain after the war.

The years immediately following the war did not bring relief from restrictions and rationing. Indeed, during the late 1940s, shortages actually became more severe. Britain's economy went through a series of major difficulties. Individuals were asked to 'tighten their belts' even more than in wartime. The British people not only had to 'make do and mend' when it came to small luxuries; they also reached new lows in basics such as fuel. Even the weather added to the misery as these drab, shortage-plagued years were hit by one of the worst winters this century, during January and February 1947.

From where were 300,000 Allied soldiers rescued by a fleet of destroyers, ferries, fishing boats and pleasure cruisers?

Dunkirk (on the northern coast of France)

In May the Germans invaded Belgium, Holland and France. Their *blitzkrieg* attacks overwhelmed the armies of these countries, together with the British Expeditionary Force. The defeated armies were encircled at Dunkirk. A fleet of small vessels crossed the Channel to rescue them from the beaches. Many ships were destroyed as the rescue fleet was bombed. A small rearguard fought to hold up the enemy until the evacuation was complete. Although defeated, Britain had saved most of its expeditionary force to fight another day.

Which historic building was destroyed in an air-raid on Coventry on 14 November?

St Michael's, the old cathedral

Only the great tower and its spire remained intact. A cold, clear night provided ideal conditions for the German bombers. A total of 50,000 homes and 500 shops were also destroyed. The widespread damage led to a major reconstruction of the city. This included a new cathedral, designed by Basil Spence. The new St Michael's was built against the ruins of the old and was consecrated in 1962. The city centre was eventually reconstructed using pedestrian precincts, a new idea at the time.

Who became Prime Minister in May, following Chamberlain's resignation?

Winston Churchill

On 7 May, Chamberlain had opened a two-day debate on the Norwegian campaign in the House of Commons. The handling of the fighting in Norway had left a lot to be desired and the blame for this failure had been placed on Chamberlain. This was not entirely fair, as most of the bad decisions made during the Norwegian campaign had been made by other people (including Churchill). Nevertheless many of Chamberlain's usual supporters now voted against him and also made it clear that they would only support the government if Labour and Liberals were brought in as well. It was unlikely that the other parties would accept such a coalition with Chamberlain as Prime Minister. After Chamberlain resigned on 10 May, Churchill was duly appointed as Prime Minister and Britain's war leader.

Which capital city was occupied by the Germans on 14 June?

Paris

Which Northern comedian appeared in Somewhere in England?

Frank Randle

Randle was a crude Music Hall performer whose act was mainly about beer, girls and rude noises. He made nine films in all. His *Somewhere* series came in the early 1940s: *Somewhere in England*, *Somewhere in Camp* (1942), *Somewhere on Leave* (1942) and *Somewhere in Civvies* (1943). His stage act was toned down for the camera. The sort of humour his films contained is illustrated by the scene where Randle is on the parade ground riding a donkey. "What do you think you're doing?", demands the Colonel. "Ah'm sittin' on me ass", replies Randle. A catch-phrase of Randle's was "Get off me foot."

Who sang When You Wish Upon A Star *in a movie this year?*

Jiminy Cricket (in Walt Disney's *Pinocchio*)

Pinocchio was Disney's best-drawn cartoon. It used a multi-plane Technicolour process that proved too expensive to repeat in other films. Based on Carlo Collodi's story, it tells how the old puppet-maker, Geppetto, makes a boy puppet which is brought to life by the Blue Fairy (to the accompaniment of *When You Wish Upon A Star*). Pinocchio becomes aware of all sorts of human desires and temptations which are reflected in the behaviour of his monstrous nose. As well as Jiminy Cricket, Pinocchio's other new friends include Figaro the cat and Cleo the confident goldfish.

Which American big-band leader had a hit with I'll Never Smile Again *this year?*

Tommy Dorsey

Dorsey was one of the most successful leaders in the American big-band era. His brother, Jimmy, was also a band-leader. In 1935 Tommy formed his own band, whose theme tune was *I'm Getting Sentimental Over You*. Other songs associated with Dorsey include *Treasure Island* (vocal by Edythe Wright), *Alone, Marie, In The Blue Of The Evening* (vocal by Frank Sinatra) and *On the Sunny Side of the Street*. Tommy Dorsey died after an accidental combination of liquor and sleeping pills following a large meal in 1956.

What new radio series broadcast twice daily, at 10.30 am and 10.30 pm (for the night-shift)?

Music While You Work

What were taken down from around many town squares, parks and cemeteries to help the war effort?

Wrought iron railings

The collection of salvage became a familiar activity for most wartime households. Especially needed were waste paper, cardboard, scrap metal and bones. Britain could no longer import all the goods it had in peacetime. The dangers to shipping meant that other sources of materials had to be looked for. Salvage was one such area. Drives such as Saucepans into Spitfires were organized to encourage collectors to gather particular types of salvage.

Why did it become difficult to find your way around the South of England in June?

Road direction signs were taken down

At this time fears of a German invasion were at their greatest. France had been occupied and the defeated British army brought back from Dunkirk. Many people now expected the victorious Germans to move against Britain. Invasion precautions became a common sight for many. Barbed wire and land mines were laid on beaches. Concrete defences (pill boxes) were built at important points (beaches, road junctions). Obstacles were placed on roads and in fields where transport aircraft might land.

Not only road signs were removed. Station place names were taken down, along with other signs which might help the invader. These measures caused some confusion. In the blackout rail travellers sometimes found it difficult to tell where they were.

Where would an Anderson shelter be found?

In the garden

Some two and a quarter million of these air-raid shelters were erected. The Anderson was sunk about four feet into the ground and had earth piled over its curved roof. It provided very good protection for up to six people but was also a most uncomfortable place to spend the night.

The Morrison shelter was a later type. It was a steel table-like structure which people could lie underneath. This provided shelter indoors. Both the Anderson and the Morrison were named after the Home Secretary of the day. Many families in blitzed areas spent long periods in such shelters. Some public brick shelters were also available but most people preferred their own (if they had one). A large number simply hid under the stairs during raids.

Where could you no longer get married in a hurry as a result of changes in Scottish Marriage Law which came into effect on 1 July?

Gretna Green

*As who did the Local Defence
Volunteers become better known?*

The Home Guard

A radio broadcast in May 1940 asked for recruits to join the LDV. The age limits were officially 17 and 65 but many older and younger people joined. It was primarily a volunteer force of young lads, men unable to join the forces for health reasons and those too old for the services. They undertook duties such as manning anti-aircraft guns. The LDV were renamed the Home Guard by Churchill. At first many Home Guard units had to drill without rifles or uniforms. Broomsticks and armbands took their place until proper equipment, much of it outdated, could be found.

*Who was William Joyce better known as
to radio listeners?*

Lord Haw Haw

Joyce was a traitor of Irish–American birth who broadcast from Germany in an effort to weaken British morale. Nearly a third of Britain listened to him regularly, mostly for amusement, though his remarks could prove worrying — as when he described how ships had been lost or where air-raids had taken place. Haw Haw's polished accent introduced his broadcasts with the famous words, "Germany Calling, Germany Calling." After the war Joyce was executed for treason.

*Who was Churchill describing when he
said "Never was so much owed by so
many to so few"?*

The RAF pilots who fought in the Battle of Britain

Between August and October, RAF pilots (and a number of Polish airmen) clashed with German bombers and fighters as they tried to destroy strategic airfields in southern England. This was an essential preliminary to any invasion of Britain. The RAF's victory in the air was a major factor in preventing German landings.

*Who were rescued from aboard the
German tanker* Altmark *in a daring raid
by a Royal Navy boarding party?*

300 British sailors held as prisoners of war

Which German battleship was sunk in the North Atlantic after what was, at the time, the biggest naval chase ever?

The *Bismarck*

Germany's newest and fastest battleship had caused a great deal of damage to Atlantic convoys. The *Bismarck* became involved in a three-day chase with the Royal Navy after it had sunk HMS *Hood*, a British battle-cruiser. Crucial damage to the rudder of the German ship was caused by aircraft from the carrier HMS *Ark Royal*.

Where did Japanese warplanes make a surprise attack on 7 December?

Pearl Harbor (Hawaii)

This was the home base of the American Pacific Fleet. Planes from Japanese carriers sank five battleships, 14 smaller ships and destroyed 200 aircraft. The United States had so far avoided becoming directly involved in the war, but had been coming into increasing conflict with Japan over Japanese expansion in South-East Asia.

The raid on Pearl Harbor brought America into the war. Britain declared war on Japan the day after the attack. With Germany and Italy declaring war upon the United States (11 December) the war became truly world-wide

Which two ships were sunk by the Japanese on 10 December?

The battleship HMS *Prince of Wales* and the battle-cruiser HMS *Repulse*

These ships had been at Singapore when the Japanese had attacked Pearl Harbor and Britain had entered the war against them on the United States' side. The Japanese had subsequently invaded nearby Malaya and, by overrunning its airfields, deprived the big ships of the air cover they had to have. Once again it was to be shown that the battleship was a weapon from another age when Japanese bombers attacked the two great ships and sank them in two hours. Six hundred men perished. The loss of prestigious capital ships in this way came as a heavy blow to a public brought up to believe that Britannia rules the waves.

What major Eastern European country did German troops invade along a 1,800-mile front on 22 June?

The Soviet Union

Who was Walt Disney's silent, flying elephant?

Dumbo

Dumbo remains one of Disney's most popular films. It tells the story of a dumb circus elephant who learns how to fly. His tutors are a group of crows (who at one point sing, *When I see an Elephant Fly*).

With the United States entering the war in December 1941, Disney spent most of the war years making propaganda and training films.

What was the Navy, Army and Air Force Institute better known as?

The NAAFI

The organization which became known as 'NAAFI' was founded in 1921 but came into its own during the Second World War. Around 38,000 NAAFI girls served in canteens at army camps, naval shore bases and RAF stations, at home and abroad. They also ran 300 mobile canteens which brought comforts to isolated units. Canteens were frequently referred to as 'the NAAFI'.

Which all-girl singing group did Patty, Maxine and Laverne make up?

The Andrews Sisters

The sisters were an American act who became known for hits such as *Don't Sit Under the Apple Tree* (with anyone else but me), *Rum and Coca-Cola*, *The Coffee Song* and *I'll Be With You* (in apple blossom time). They also appeared in various movies, including three Abbott and Costello comedies in 1941.

What sort of band did Primo Scala have?

An accordion band

What did you have to do in the blackout?

Cover any visible lights

The blackout was meant to make it harder for German bombers to identify their position over Britain. Windows (of factories, homes, etc) had to be covered up when inside lights were on. Blackout curtains and screens were fitted before lights went on. Street lighting was restricted and car headlights were masked (this caused many road accidents).

The nine months from September 1940 to May 1941 saw the period of bombing referred to as the Blitz take place. London, Liverpool, Hull, Coventry, Bristol, Belfast and Birmingham were among the targets. When an air-raid was over, the sirens would sound the all-clear. Vera Lynn recorded a popular song entitled, *When They Sound the Last All-clear.*

What type of oil was issued to children under two in the vitamin welfare scheme which began in 1941?

Cod liver oil (rich in vitamins A and D)

Blackcurrant juice (later orange juice) — rich in vitamin C — was also issued under the scheme. Cod liver oil is remembered by many for its unpleasant taste. Interestingly, only 49 per cent of those entitled took up these benefits. The most dangerous period of the war for civilians produced a number of such welfare measures. Cheap milk was also instituted for children and expectant mothers.

Young children were allowed half the adult amount of meat. Christmas brought a little extra sugar and sweets.

What did you need, as well as money, to buy clothes after 2 June?

Clothing coupons

Clothes now joined food on the ration. The basic rate of 66 coupons was intended to cover one complete outfit a year. Make do and mend were wartime watchwords. Old outfits were handed down and altered, often being used to create a completely different type of garment, such as a new skirt from a worn-out coat.

Utility clothes first appeared in 1941. Material was saved through the use of smaller hems, fewer pockets and other extras. The designs were plain and simple, though the cloth used was of reasonable quality. Garments were labelled CC41 (Clothing Control 1941).

Why did many men and women have to enrol to patrol their workplaces on several nights each month?

To act as firewatchers

Which Hollywood star was famous for her exotic costumes and 'tutti-frutti' hats?

Carmen Miranda

Known as the Brazilian Bombshell (though she was actually born in Portugal), Miranda appeared in a number of musicals over the 1940s. These included *Down Argentine Way* (1940), *That Night in Rio* (1941) and *Weekend in Havana* (1941). Miranda did not have large parts in most of the movies she appeared in. She would come on at intervals in one of her spectacular costumes to perform a big latin number in her extravagant way. One of the best known of these was *I, Yi, Yi, Yi, Yi, (I Like You Very Much)*.

Which VIP parachuted into Scotland on 10 May?

Rudolf Hess, Hitler's deputy

No-one knows why Hess flew to Britain. He claimed at the time to have an important message for the Duke of Hamilton. Rumours of possible peace overtures began when news of his arrival was broken. This suggestion was rejected by both the British and German governments. The Nazis claimed that Hess was unstable and suffering from hallucinations. After the war Hess was to plead insanity in his trial at Nuremberg (though his claim was not accepted). He received a sentence of life imprisonment and died at Spandau in 1987.

Who played Mrs Miniver?

Greer Garson

This popular, Oscar-winning film provided a rose-tinted, far from realistic view of what life was like in wartime Britain. Greer Garson played the plucky, resourceful and ever-cheerful Mrs Miniver who was winning through despite hardship. This Hollywood view of the war was typical in that those films that did recognize the war did so in this morale-boosting style. The vast majority of wartime films had nothing to do with the war and met the audience's need for escapist distraction at a difficult time.

Who was the Minister of Food in Churchill's administration?

Lord Woolton

Where did 60,000 British soldiers surrender on 15 February?

Singapore

This was the biggest surrender in British history. Singapore had its defences somewhat neglected in the early years of the war as forces were needed elsewhere. While Japan stayed out of the war, Singapore inevitably fell in the list of priorities. All this had to change after Pearl Harbor. Japanese troops advanced down the Malayan Peninsula to attack the island fortress. This revealed the fundamental weakness of the island's defences. Singapore was defended by ships when it needed fighter aircraft. The loss of Singapore was considered a huge blow to British prestige. It was also considered, at the time, to be a severe blow to the war effort (the effects of its loss proved exaggerated in the long term). To those living at the time, this was a low point for British fortunes and morale.

What rang for the first time since 1940 in November?

Church bells

The ringing of bells had been stopped in 1940 when the threat of German invasion was at its greatest. They were only to be sounded as a warning if the invader came. By 1942 the invasion threat had diminished. In the first significant victory won by the British, the Eighth Army under Montgomery proved too strong for Rommel's Afrika Korps at El Alamein. The regular ringing of church bells was resumed in April 1943.

What was the last food to go on ration during the war?

Sweets

In July the last extension of rationing during the war meant that each person could buy up to 8oz of chocolate and sweets a month (raised to 12oz in October). Sweet rationing went on until 1953. (1954 saw the end of all rationing.)

To which Mediterranean island did the King award a George Cross in April?

Malta

What seasonal favourite was first sung in the film Holiday Inn?

White Christmas

Popular 'crooner' Bing Crosby was one of the stars of this wartime film. This was his first performance of the Irving Berlin song with which he was always to be associated.

Which song became a favourite of both German and British soldiers in North Africa?

Lili Marlene

This German song was popular with the Afrika Korps (the German Army in North Africa commanded by General Rommel). The British Eighth Army listened in to German radio and adopted the song. The first English recording was made by Anne Shelton. It was also recorded by Vera Lynn, Marlene Dietrich and Lale Anderson.

What famous gangster movie star won an Oscar for the musical Yankee Doodle Dandy?

Jimmy Cagney

Cagney's reputation as an actor was based mainly on the many gangster movies he made during the 1930s. However in his long film career he was not restricted to gangster roles. *The Oklahoma Kid* (1939) was his first Western and *The Strawberry Blonde* (1941) was a romance with Olivia de Havilland.

What did the initials ENSA stand for?

Entertainments National Services Association

What was supposed to be no more than five inches deep from this year?

Bathwater

Keeping clean was becoming more difficult. The fuel shortage meant that people were urged to take fewer baths and to run no more than five inches of water. Lines were painted on baths in hotels and public baths to show the correct level. Bathwater was frequently shared.

To make things more difficult, soap was rationed (one tablet every four weeks). In 1944, *Lifebuoy* Toilet Soap was being advertised at 3½d (thruppence ha'penny) per tablet, together with one coupon. Razor blades were even harder to obtain and men tried to make them last by running them around the inside of a glass tumbler.

What sort of egg, milk and potato was now imported from America?

These were all imported as dried foods

Dried foods made best use of the limited shipping space available. Atlantic convoys suffered greatly from German submarine attacks and many merchant ships were lost.

Dried foods provided a boost to people's dwindling food rations. When reconstituted for use in cooking, 4oz of dried egg was the equivalent of nine large eggs.

Why did some working women take to putting their hair up with a headscarf or turban?

As a safety measure to keep their hair out of factory machines

The shortage of material available for hats also encouraged the popularity of the headscarf. An important advantage was its ability to cover a multitude of pins in an emergency. Snoods were also much worn, again mainly for practical reasons. These were a type of hair net but made of thicker material and worn towards the back of the head. They held up loose long hair.

Since 1942 women too had been conscripted into essential war work. A minority joined the women's branches of the services. Most went into essential industries. These included aircraft factories, shipyards and munitions works. Women found themselves in many previously all-male workplaces.

What colour was a child's (under 6) ration book?

Green

Which British singer's first radio series was called Introducing Anne?

Anne Shelton

The tune she sang at the start of these programmes was *Lili Marlene* (which she was the first to record with English lyrics). Anne Shelton was popular throughout the 1940s and early 1950s. Many of her records were big sellers; these included *My Yiddishe Momme, I'll Be Seeing You, Galway Bay, Village of St Bernadette* and *Lay Down Your Arms.*

Who almost said "Play it again, Sam" in the movie Casablanca?

Humphrey Bogart

What he actually said was, "You played it for her, play it for me." The tune he wanted to hear was *As Time Goes By*. Bogart made many films over his long career, often playing private detectives or gangsters. His best-known movies include *High Sierra* (1941), *To Have and Have Not* (1944), *The Big Sleep* (1946) and *The African Queen* (1951). His third wife was Lauren Bacall, who starred in several of his movies.

Who did the Germans install as Prime Minister of Norway in February?

Vidkun Quisling

Norway had been invaded by the Germans early on in the war (April 1940). The German forces had quickly overcome the resistance of the Norwegians and a British expeditionary force. The Norwegian government and King Haakon came to London. A million tons of shipping and several thousand servicemen also came to Britain from Norway. Quisling had been a collaborator since these early days and was now given his reward by the Nazis who made him their puppet Prime Minister. Quisling's name has since entered the English language as a term for a traitor. He was later sentenced to death for treason and shot on 24 October 1945.

Who was the blonde movie star with 'million dollar legs' that became the favourite pin-up for US servicemen during the war?

Betty Grable

Who were the Bevin Boys?

Conscripted miners

The shortage of miners prompted Ernest Bevin (Minister of Labour) to direct young men to work in the mines. From the end of 1943, 10 per cent of young men reaching conscription age were chosen by ballot as Bevin Boys. A draw was made at intervals of the numbers 0 to 9 and those men whose national service registration certificates happened to end with the selected figure were transferred to coal mining. Some 45,000 found themselves in this unpopular service. Most of them worked on haulage and maintenance, as many found it difficult to keep up with experienced miners on the coal face.

What was the only part of Britain to be occupied by Germany?

The Channel Islands

The British government had decided not to defend the Islands in June 1940. The Germans had turned them into fortresses by 1943 and the occupation went on until the end of the war.

Which country declared war on Germany on 13 October?

Italy

The Allies invaded Sicily in July and were on the Italian mainland by 17 August. Mussolini had been deposed in July and the Italian will to resist was weakening daily. The new Italian government signed an armistice on 8 September. This did not mean the end of the fighting for the Allies as the German troops in Italy provided fierce resistance during their retreat.

The Italians completed a wartime turnaround with their declaration of war on their former allies. Following Italy's surrender, the retreating German soldiers had indulged in looting and atrocities against the Italian population.

At what Russian city did Field Marshal von Paulus surrender a German army on 31 January, after one of the war's most ferocious battles?

Stalingrad

What did the letters ITMA stand for?

It's That Man Again (broadcast 1939 to 1949)

This wartime radio comedy series starred the Liverpudlian comedian Tommy Handley. *ITMA* featured comic characters such as Mrs Mopp, with her catch-phrase, "Can I do you now sir?" Around 16 million people tuned in to *ITMA*. The show's other catch-phrases included "It's being so cheerful as keeps me going", "Well, I'll go to the foot of our stairs" and "TTFN" (ta ta for now). The last *ITMA* broadcast was in January 1949. Tommy Handley died three days later.

What wartime radio programme provided lunch-time music and entertainment for factory workers?

Workers' Playtime

Beginning in 1941, this show was broadcast direct from a factory 'somewhere in England'. The regular compere was Bill Gates. Frequent appearances were made by Elsie and Doris Waters as Gert and Daisy. The show continued long after the war, the final broadcast being made in 1964.

Who began to chase Jerry the Mouse in the early 1940s?

Tom, the cat, in the MGM cartoon series, *Tom and Jerry*

In the 1940s many new cartoon series began to rival the popularity of Disney's work. The cat and mouse pursuits of Tom and Jerry featured in short cartoons which are still shown regularly on the television. Other studios also produced successful cartoon series. Warners gave us Woody Woodpecker and Sylvester the cat with his intended victim Tweety Pie. Warners' best-known cartoon character was, and still is, Bugs Bunny, with his catch-phrase, "What's up, Doc?"

What popular film did MGM produce, featuring an 11-year-old Elizabeth Taylor, Roddy McDowall and a collie?

Lassie Come Home

What did careless talk cost, according to a well-known wartime poster?

Careless Talk Costs Lives

This was one of several slogans warning against giving away valuable information (such as where your husband had been posted) in idle chatter. Another poster advised, 'Be Like Dad — Keep Mum.' The Ministry of Information produced a huge amount of advice, propaganda and instruction during the war, much of which was ignored. Another of the best-known slogans advised that 'Walls Have Ears'.

What centre-piece was missing from wedding celebrations after July?

The traditional iced wedding cake

Food shortages led to a ban on the making and selling of this wedding centre-piece. The Whited Sepulchre became a feature of many wartime weddings; this was a hollow, cardboard or satin model of a large wedding cake. Inside there would be a small cake, usually made with dried egg, gravy browning and rum essence. Rationing and shortages meant that wartime weddings were mostly modest affairs. Material was difficult to find for wedding outfits and food and drink were hard to provide for receptions.

What was the only type of new furniture being made from 1943 onwards?

Utility furniture

Furniture and household goods (eg. bedding, kitchen tools, prams) were very hard to obtain. Utility furniture was limited in materials and simple in design. Priority for licences to buy the furniture was given to people bombed out or to couples setting up home.

What apologetic notice was frequently to be found outside pubs during the war years?

Sorry, No Beer

As what radio figure was Charles Hill better known?

The Radio Doctor

Health tips from the Radio Doctor were included in the *Kitchen Front* broadcasts made by the Ministry of Food. These came after the 8.00 am news and aimed at encouraging people to make the best use of their rations and to eat healthily. Shortages and rationing meant that people used a range of unusual foods to supplement their diet. Housewives made fatless pastry, eggless cakes and sugarless puddings. The Radio Doctor frequently promoted the virtues of tripe, a food which had previously only been popular in the North of England.

What army worked on the farms to help produce food?

The Land Army

This brought thousands of women and girls onto the farms, many of whose workers had been conscripted into the services. Evacuees and Italian prisoners of war also helped in the fields. Apart from milking and care of livestock, Land Army girls were employed as tractor drivers and general farm hands.

Who was rescued by German paratroopers on 12 September?

Mussolini

The Italian dictator had been deposed in July, when Marshal Badoglio had become Prime Minister and chief of the government. Mussolini had been imprisoned by the new regime. After the new Italian government had signed an armistice with the Allies, the *duce* was rescued from his captivity in a behind-the-lines operation carried out by German paratroopers.

Mussolini's freedom lasted until April 1945, when he was captured by Italian partisans. The Fascist dictator met his end when he and his mistress, Clara Petacci, were shot and strung up by their heels on a garage forecourt in Milan.

Which scantily-clad cartoon character was drawn for the Daily Mirror *by Norman Pett?*

Jane

What new threat was launched on London in June?

The V1 flying bomb (the 'doodlebug' or 'buzz-bomb')

Over 10,000 of these slow, noisy, pilotless planes were launched against London and the South-East over a 10-month period at the end of the war. This unexpected final wave of air attacks began on 12 June, a week after D-Day. The longer-range V2 rocket bombs began to fall in September. They gave little warning of their approach, unlike the V1s which could be heard (its engine would cut out just before it fell). Both carried large loads of high explosive and caused many civilian casualties in London and the South-East. The final V2 fell on the Tottenham Court Road in March 1945.

What day was 6 June to become better known as?

D-Day

In the biggest combined land, sea and air operation of all time, British, American and Canadian troops were landed on the beaches of Normandy, in northern France. This began the long-awaited Allied invasion of Western Europe. At the start of the operation, RAF and American bombers made continual raids on German defences and communications. The first soldiers to land were airborne troops who were dropped behind enemy lines by parachute or glider. Several thousand ships brought the main force across the Channel and landing craft took them to five main beach heads.

The overall commander of the operation was the American General Eisenhower. The Russians had long been asking its Western allies to open a Second Front in Europe. They had lost millions of men in their fight to drive the invading Germans out of the Soviet Union.

Where was a battle fought around a hilltop monastery?

Monte Cassino in Italy

The Allies invaded Italy in 1943. Their advance was held up when German troops fortified the Benedictine monastery at Monte Cassino. It proved very difficult to dislodge the Germans. Although the Allies tried to avoid needless damage of historic buildings, the threat to the attacking forces led them to bomb Cassino, using American Flying Fortresses.

Monte Cassino was finally taken in May 1944, when it was stormed by British and Polish troops. Rome was captured in June 1944, although the retreating Germans went on fighting in the North of Italy.

Where did British paratroopers attempt to capture a bridge over the Rhine during September?

Arnhem

Which three Hollywood stars went on the Road to Utopia?

Crooner Bing Crosby, comedian Bob Hope and the glamorous Dorothy Lamour

In 1940 Singapore became the first of the destinations in the very popular *Road to . . .* comedies made during the 1940s. The trio also went to Zanzibar (1941), Morocco (1942) and Rio (1947). The blend of comedy and songs from the three stars proved hugely popular during these troubled years.

What colour was Rita Hayworth's hair?

Red

Hayworth was one of Hollywood's best-known redheads (though her hair had been black until she dyed it for a part in *The Strawberry Blonde* in 1941). Several of her films were musicals; as a dancer she partnered Fred Astaire and Gene Kelly. Hayworth movies included *Cover Girl* (1944) and *Gilda* (1946). Hayworth married film star Orson Welles and later the multi-millionaire Prince Aly Khan (1949).

What was the 'Jitterbug'?

A dance

During the war dancing was very popular as it was simple to organize. People danced in canteens, service camps, village halls and the big palais de danse. A conventional dance would have included quicksteps, foxtrots and a last waltz. This rather sedate activity was in contrast to the energetic new dance styles which arrived with the Americans. The jitterbug became popular with some of the younger dancers, though their lively styles annoyed many and they were banned in several dance-halls.

What popular film did MGM produce, featuring a 12-year-old Elizabeth Taylor, Mickey Rooney and a horse?

National Velvet

Why were American troops called GIs?

Because all of their equipment was stamped Government Issue

The numbers of GIs in Britain reached a peak in the months before D-Day (6 June). The quality of their equipment was much higher than that available to British servicemen. America's greater wealth showed itself in the flashy uniforms it provided for its troops. A British soldier might expect to sit in a draughty canteen, drinking hot tea and eating a rock cake made with reconstituted egg. An American marine would have plentiful coffee, doughnuts and ice-cream.

Complete this question from a familiar poster, seen at railway stations: Is your journey . . .

Really necessary?

Passenger trains were very overcrowded during the war because of the shortage of rolling stock. Passengers often had to travel in corridors and carriages were blacked out. Coal shortages also affected the railways. Large numbers of servicemen were having to be transported by the country's rail network. Inessential journeys by civilians were therefore discouraged to help ease the movement of servicemen and supplies.

As what was Supply pressed American meat better known?

Spam

Spam and corned beef began to be imported from America under the lend-lease agreement. These tinned meats were available under the points rationing system, which left the customers free to choose what to spend their points on each month. They were used to eke out the meat ration. People ate them in Spam fritters or as Corned beef hash.

What were people asked to Dig For . . . in a wartime poster?

Victory

Which popular American band leader went missing when his aircraft was lost over the English Channel in December?

Glen Miller

Miller's American Air Force Band was famous for its 'swing' arrangements, including *In the Mood, Moonlight Serenade* and *Chattanooga Choo-Choo*. Miller was a favourite of the American servicemen now in Britain, his music often being featured on the American Forces Network radio.

Who were Alvar Lidell, Bruce Belfrage, Joseph MacLeod and Frank Philips?

Newsreaders

The radio news was easily the most listened to of the BBC's programmes during the war. The chimes of Big Ben were followed by the introduction, "Here is the news and this is Alvar Lidell [for example] reading it." Newsreaders had begun to identify themselves as a precaution against the use of radio in an enemy takeover. Previously the news had been delivered by an anonymous voice. Bruce Belfrage gained attention because he carried on reading the news when a bomb exploded in Broadcasting House.

For nearly everyone, the radio was the most important source of information during the war. The tiny British television service had been closed down for the duration. Newspapers could not reach such a large audience as quickly as the radio. They were also badly affected by the paper shortage which greatly reduced the number of their pages.

Where were Anzac soldiers from?

Australia and New Zealand

During the war people became used to meeting a range of foreigners hardly seen in pre-war Britain. The first to arrive had been refugee soldiers from the occupied countries of Europe. These included units of Polish, Czech, Free French, Belgian, Dutch and Norwegian servicemen. The Dominions of Australia, New Zealand and Canada entered the war within a week of its declaration and large numbers of their soldiers were also stationed in Britain.

Which young Jewish diarist was discovered in her hiding-place in occupied Amsterdam this year?

Anne Frank

What did VE Day stand for?

Victory in Europe Day

The war in Europe came to an end in the early hours of 8 May 1945. This was when the surrender document was signed in Berlin. Churchill announced the victory over Germany in a radio broadcast to the country. They days of 8 and 9 May were declared public holidays in celebration, with 8 May known as VE Day. The news sparked off celebrations all over the country. Flags, streamers and bunting (if any could be found) decorated the streets and victory parties were held.

One group of people who could not celebrate fully were the families of servicemen still fighting in the Far East. Victory over Japan was not to arrive for another 100 days — 14 August 1945.

What fell on Hiroshima on 6 August?

An atomic bomb

The newly developed atomic bomb destroyed the thriving Japanese city of Hiroshima. The raid was carried out by an American Super-Fortress bomber. The plane which carried the Hiroshima bomb was named *Enola Gay* after the pilot's mother.

A second A-bomb was dropped three days later upon the ship-building city of Nagasaki. This killed 70,000 people as the city was covered by the bomb's characteristic mushroom-shaped cloud. Five days later (14 August) Japan surrendered unconditionally to the Allies.

Who went on trial at Nuremberg during November?

A group of Nazi war leaders

A number of prominent figures from Hitler's regime were brought before a tribunal formed by Britain, America, the Soviet Union and France. Amongst those in the dock at Nuremberg's Palace of Justice were Goering, Hess, Ribbentrop, Keitel, Doenitz, Streicher and von Papen. The charges were: waging a war of aggression, violating the laws and customs of warfare and crimes against humanity. Only Hans Frank, Nazi governor of Poland, pleaded guilty. Of the group 12 were sentenced to death (though Goering cheated the hangman by taking cyanide and Martin Bormann was tried 'in absentia'). The remaining 10 were executed in October 1946.

Which three Allied leaders met at Yalta in the Crimea during February?

Roosevelt, Stalin and Churchill

Who hosted the BBC Dancing Club?

Victor Silvester and his orchestra

The Dancing Club was a long-running mixture of dance, instruction and strict-tempo dance music by Silvester. The first lesson, broadcast in 1941, had been for the quickstep, with the instruction, 'slow, slow, quick-quick, slow' becoming a national catch-phrase. The signature tune was Silvester's own *You're Dancing on My Heart*.

What replaced the Forces Programme on 1500 metres?

The Light Programme

The BBC's entertainment alternative to the Home Service replaced the Forces Programme on Sunday 29 July 1945. The signature tune was *Oranges and Lemons* followed by Big Ben chiming 9 o'clock, the news and Sandy MacPhearson at the Theatre Organ. The Light Programme was replaced by Radio 2 on 30 September 1967.

Who was Bud Abbott's partner in many 1940s comedy films?

Lou Costello

Abbott and Costello were American comedians who made many low-budget films during the 1940s and early 1950s. Their movies followed a similar pattern, with titles such as *Abbott and Costello in Hollywood* (1945) and *Abbott and Costello Meet Frankenstein* (1948). Bud Abbott was the straight man with the small, fat, baby-faced Costello providing the comic character. Their films were not particularly inventive but they became very familiar to cinema audiences in the late 1940s, especially as B movies in support of the main feature.

Which two-way broadcasts between London and Germany began on 7 October?

Family Favourites

What sort of leg-wear became more common for women in the war years?

Trousers and Slacks

The wearing of trousers amongst women was not widespread before the war. However the numbers of women now working in factories, on the land and as drivers brought a demand for such a comfortable, functional fashion. The need to spend time in air-raid shelters also made such a warm garment popular. At first trousers were fairly wide and loose fitting but later they became narrower and tapered.

What did some women draw on the back of their legs because of the scarcity of stockings?

A black line

Some women met the stocking shortage by using leg make-up. This might be home-made, using ingredients like gravy browning. Some commercially produced lotions were available. Before a night out, legs were painted and a black line drawn up the back, usually with an eye pencil, to look like a seam. Cosmetics were in very short supply during the war. This was made more inconvenient because the pre-war fashion had been for quite heavy make-up. Women used their imagination to find replacements: soot could be used as mascara and beetroot juice served as lipstick. Cosmetics were also available on the black market, though their ingredients were often rather dubious.

What sort of outfit did many servicemen wear on leaving the forces?

A demob suit

The demob suit with which men left the forces became a common sight. In August, 171,000 servicemen a month were being demobilized and returning home. Demob suits were not very stylish. However they were well made and, unlike wartime utility suits, jackets had inside breast pockets and side pockets with flaps. Trousers again had turn-ups and could also have three pockets. Some family men used demob coupons to buy children's clothing, which was in very short supply.

What were Camels *and* Lucky Strike?

American cigarettes

Who replaced Winston Churchill as Prime Minister after the 5 July General Election?

Clement Attlee

The wartime coalition government had broken up after the German surrender in May. An election was called for July, the first to be held since 1935. The result of the 1945 General Election was a big victory for the Labour Party. Britain's wartime Prime Minister, Winston Churchill, was rejected as a peacetime leader. Many soldiers, sailors and airmen voted from far-flung postings.

The leading figures in the new Labour government were Attlee, Herbert Morrison (Home Secretary and Deputy Prime Minister) and Ernie Bevin (Foreign Secretary).

Who married Eva Braun on 29 April?

Adolf Hitler

As Russian soldiers advanced on Berlin, Hitler spent his last days in his underground fortress, issuing orders to armies which had long since disintegrated. His close followers, including Goering and Himmler, had fled from Berlin. On 29 April, Hitler married his mistress, Eva Braun. The following day Braun took poison and Hitler shot himself.

Who was known for the catch-phrase 'Four n'arf, Tish'?

Cheerful Charlie Chester

Tish and Tosh were a pair of spivs played by Chester and Len Marten. They appeared in *Studio Stand Easy*, the army section of the wartime programme *Merry-Go-Round*. Their duologue began with 'Wotcher Tish, Wotcher Tosh'. Chester was also known for singing *The Old Bazaar In Cairo*. After the war, *Stand Easy* became a civvy series in its own right. Charlie Chester's other radio work included shows such as *Come to Charlie* and *The Charlie Chester Show*.

Who was Hitler's successor as German leader for the last days of the war?

Admiral Doenitz

Where were 33 people killed watching an FA Cup semi-final in March?

Burnden Park, Bolton

On 9 March, Bolton Wanderers played Stoke City in an FA Cup semi-final. The Bolton ground was filled by a very large crowd. Overcrowding had been made a little worse because part of the ground was closed on account of fire hazards. At the ground's Railway End enclosure the overcrowding was at its worst. When hundreds more spectators forced their way in after the turnstiles had been locked, the overcrowding grew too great. Barriers collapsed and people piled on top of each other. A stream of ambulances ferried people to hospital. In addition to the 33 dead, 500 were injured. Just over 40 years later a very similar incident was to take place at Hillsborough in Sheffield.

How much was the new family allowance?

Five shillings a week

The Allowance was given to the second child and to subsequent ones up to the age of 15 (or 16 if in full-time education). A young Barbara Castle described the allowance as a 'paltry sum'. Children's allowances, maternity and death benefits had not existed in pre-war Britain. The new Labour Government introduced a range of new welfare benefits through the National Insurance Act of 1946 (though the child allowance had been put forward by Churchill's caretaker government).

The 1946 National Insurance Act established a new system of unemployment pay which did not rely on a means test of collective family income.

What did a horse called Lovely Cottage win on 5 April?

The first Grand National since 1940

Britain had now begun to return to peacetime activities. The Derby, back at Epsom after six years, was won by Airbourne in June.

What life-saving drug, used with soldiers during the war, was now announced as soon to be freely available?

Penicillin

Which special agent made his debut at 6.45 pm on Monday 7 October?

Dick Barton

Dick Barton – Special Agent was the first daily serial broadcast by the BBC. It was a fast-moving adventure series popular with youngsters. Several series were put together, with the final episode being broadcast in 1951. Other characters included Snowy White and Jock Anderson.

How did 950,000 men spend their Saturday afternoon, for the first time since 1940, on 1 September?

Watching a league football match

This was the first full football league programme to be played since the 1939/40 season. The game had not stopped altogether during the war but many footballers were in the services and a number of football grounds were used for war work. Arsenal's ground, Highbury, was used as a Civil Defence Base.

Crowds were very large. Six clubs attracted gates of over 50,000 spectators for these first matches since the war. A highlight of the day was the 6–1 thrashing of Arsenal by Wolves.

In which radio quiz show was Mabel at the table and Barney told to "Give 'em the money"?

Have a Go

This popular show was hosted by Wilfred Pickles. He travelled all over England facing people with an interview and a short quiz. The quiz questions would pay off at: (1) half-a-crown; (2) five shillings; (3) ten shillings and (4) one pound. The jackpot winner would leave with 37/6d. The programme was first heard nationally on the Light Programme in 1946 and went on until 1961. Barney was the programme's producer.

What new, daily, record-request series was first introduced by Robert MacDermott on Monday morning, 4 March?

Housewives' Choice

What arrived at Covent Garden Market in March, for the first time since 1939?

Bananas

For some time, imported fruits such as bananas and lemons had been almost completely unavailable. Valuable shipping space had been needed for essential supplies and munitions. Produce from around the world now slowly began to reappear. The war had disrupted harvests around the world and the Merchant Navy had lost many ships to German U-boats. Poor harvests and lack of shipping meant that it would be some time before such fruit became a common sight.

What were the temporary houses called which were built to meet the housing shortage after the war?

Prefabs

During the war many houses had been destroyed in air-raids and building work had been suspended. Prefabrication was one attempt to ease the resulting housing shortage. A total of 160,000 prefabs were built and, although designed as a temporary measure, a number became permanent homes for their occupiers. The single-storey, factory-made houses were often erected on cleared bomb-sites.

A large number of wartime newly-weds were forced to live with in-laws because of this housing shortage.

What alternative uses did some women find for parachute silk after the war?

As material for curtains, table-cloths and even underwear

Continuing shortages of household goods meant that the ability to make do and mend was essential for couples setting up home. All sorts of unlikely fabrics were made into curtains, table-cloths and bed linen. Carpeting was also very difficult to obtain, though a limited range of hard-wearing felting was available.

What was billed as a new daily programme of music, advice and entertainment for the home and began on 7 October?

Woman's Hour

As who were Elsie and Doris Waters also known?

Gert and Daisy

This comedy act appeared in many concert parties and on radio. Elsie and Doris adopted the characters of Cockney housewives, Gert and Daisy. The Waters sisters' brother, Jack, went on to become better known as Jack Warner — Dixon of Dock Green.

Who was the blonde actress who co-starred with Alan Ladd in thrillers such as The Blue Dahlia *and was well known for her hairstyle?*

Veronica Lake

Veronica Lake's hairstyle became widely copied during the 1940s. Her long hair was draped to the side over one eye. She was persuaded to put her hair up for the duration of the war in order to encourage women machine operators to do the same (as a safety measure).

Lake and Ladd's 1940s thrillers included *This Gun For Hire* and *The Glass Key* — both 1942.

Which children's character now appeared on the radio at 8 pm every Tuesday (repeated Sunday afternoon)?

William (in *Just William*)

These shows had a big family audience in the late 1940s and early 1950s on radio. They later gave rise to numerous TV series. The radio series used Richmal Crompton's famous schoolboy character, but in newly-written stories. The first three broadcasts (in October 1945) had used original stories by Crompton. The success of these had prompted the introduction of the series which needed a supply of new plots. John Clark became the first radio William and the original cast also featured a young Charles Hawtrey as bad boy Hubert Lane.

Who was Hollywood's swimming star?

Esther Williams

Why was Princess Elizabeth allowed 100 extra clothing coupons this year by the Board of Trade?

To buy her wedding dress

The white satin dress had been designed by Norman Hartnell. Princess Elizabeth (now Elizabeth II) married Prince Philip at Westminster Abbey on 20 November. The bridegroom (listed in the order of service as Lieutenant Philip Mountbatten) had been given the title 'Duke of Edinburgh' by the King earlier in the day. Prince Philip of Greece had become a naturalized Briton in March.

Why were hundreds of roads blocked, trains unable to run, four million workers unable to work and whole areas without electricity for substantial periods during the first three months of this year?

Because of the severe winter

Heavy snowstorms and sub-zero temperatures had combined with a serious coal shortage to produce a crisis. On 29 January the temperature fell to -16 in places. The great freeze lasted well into March.

Two million sheep were killed and half a million acres of wheat were damaged when the thaw set in during late March and April. The Spring brought serious floods, with several towns erecting duckboards in flooded streets.

Where did British rule come to an end after 163 years in August?

India

British rule came to an end on the stroke of midnight, 14 August. Two new Dominions, India and Pakistan, were born out of Britain's Indian Empire. Lord Louis Mountbatten had been appointed as Britain's last viceroy. He had to preside over the granting of independence at a time marred by serious communal riots and violence between Hindus and Moslems. Pakistan was established as a separate Moslem state. In India Nehru's first Cabinet had been sworn in at the end of 1946.

What started up at Harwell on 15 August?

Britain's first atomic power station

Who was the comedian famous for telling stories about 'The day war broke out . . .'?

Robb Wilton

Wilton was a northern variety performer whose best-known routines were his comedy monologues as a hen-pecked husband. During the Second World War he began to introduce his act with the same ten words: "The day war broke out, my missus said to me . . ." These remained with him as a catch-phrase.

Who sang When You Were Sweet Sixteen *in 1947, having been chasing rainbows in 1946?*

The American singer, Perry Como

I'm Always Chasing Rainbows was one of Como's early hits. The melody was based upon music by the classical composer, Chopin (as had been Como's first big success *Till the End of Time* in 1945). His other big sellers in the 1940s included: *If I Loved You* (1945) and *Because* (1948).

Como had many subsequent hits in a successful singing career which went on into the 1970s.

What was an Association footballer's maximum wage increased to in this year?

£12 a week

At this time, English footballers' wages were controlled by the Football League. A maximum wage had originally been imposed in 1901 and was supposed to prevent clubs from luring players with better wages. A top-level payment of £8 per week had been in force since 1922. The new increase applied to players who had been with their clubs for five years or more.

The 1947 FA Cup Final was the first to be played since 1940. Derby County defeated Charlton Athletic 4–1 (after extra time). The League champions in the first post-war season (1946/7) were Liverpool.

Which new radio series featured Jimmy Jewel and Ben Warriss and was set at the North Pole?

Up the Pole

What was the highest for 26 years in British families this year?

The birth-rate

There were 193,865 babies born in the last quarter of 1947 alone. The raising of young families was to prove very trying for many of the new parents. One of the biggest problems faced was the shortage of suitable accommodation.

The attitudes of these post-war parents were sometimes different from those of their own parents, who had brought children up in the 1920s. This showed itself in areas such as the naming of children. The traditional habit of naming the first-born after the father/mother began to fall off. New names, like Maureen, Graham, June and Gary, began to become popular, replacing the generations of Ernests and Dorothys. Such a choice could sometimes cause a family dispute.

What was the school leaving age now raised to?

15

This change had been part of the 1944 Education Act (known as the Butler Education Act, after the Conservative politician 'Rab' Butler). This Act brought extensive changes to the education system. Previously five out of six children had received no more than an Elementary School education, to the age of 14. Now a three-tier system of Grammar Schools, Technical Schools and Secondary Moderns was introduced after the age of 11.

How many ounces did the bacon ration fall to on 9 October?

One ounce per week

The years immediately after the war were times of severe shortages. Food rations fell below wartime levels. In November 1947, potatoes were rationed to 3lb per person per week. They had not been restricted at all during the war. In March the cheese ration fell to one and a half ounces per week.

Meat, unlike other foodstuffs, was rationed by price, not weight. The weekly meat allowance now fell from 1s 2d to 1s. There was also a twopenny allowance for tinned meat (corned beef and Spam). People tightened their belts even more than they had in wartime.

What familiar figure returned to Piccadilly Circus on 28 June?

Eros

Who did Chelsea sell for a record fee of over £20,000 this year?

Tommy Lawton

Lawton was one of England's best ever centre-forwards. He scored 34 goals for Everton in 1938/9 and moved to Chelsea in 1945. His transfer in 1947 was not only newsworthy because it was the first £20,000 fee. Amazingly, Lawton moved to a Third Division club, Notts County. Lawton won 23 caps for England.

Why did Hugh Dalton make the news on 13 November?

He resigned as Chancellor of the Exchequer

Dalton's resignation came in sensational circumstances. He confessed that he had personally disclosed his Budget proposals to a journalist a few minutes before delivering his Budget speech. Dalton had been made Chancellor of the new Labour government in 1945.

Which cricketer set a new record by ending the season with 3,816 runs and 18 centuries?

Denis Compton

Compton played for Middlesex. He made his first Test appearance in 1937, at the age of 19. He was also a gifted soccer player, playing left-wing for Arsenal.

Who was the skinny, Belfast boxer who became the world flyweight champion this year?

Rinty Monaghan

Where were the 1948 Olympic Games held?

London

The London Games were held on the limited resources of Austerity Britain. There was no money available to build an Olympic stadium. Wembley Stadium was given a new cinder track and, together with the Empire Pool, formed the focus of the Games. The stars of the London Games included Emil Zatopek (the Czechoslovak who won the 10,000 metres) and the 30-year-old Dutch housewife Fanny Blankers-Koen (who won the 100 metres, 200 metres, 80 metres hurdles and 4 × 100 metres relay).

What began to provide free spectacles, dentures and prescriptions from 5 July?

The new National Health Service

One of the more lasting measures introduced by the 1945 Labour government was the bringing together of the existing forms of health care into a single National Health Service.

The new Health Service was to offer free medical treatment for the entire population. Previously the type of care available depended mainly upon a person's ability to pay. Most less well-off families paid an amount to insure themselves against sickness through hospital funds. Only a very basic service was left to those who could not afford such cover, such as those out of work for long periods. From 5 July, 2,751 hospitals were brought under the control of the new service, despite opposition from many doctors.

The realities of financing such an enormous service soon led to the introduction of charges for false teeth and spectacles in 1951.

What Middle-Eastern country was born on 14 May on the termination of the British mandate for Palestine?

Israel

Ben-Gurion became the Prime Minister of Israel's provisional government. Israel opened its doors to Jewish immigrants, who now had a national home. Arab reaction was predictable. As the last British troops were leaving, the new Israeli army was preparing to defend the new state from attack by Egyptian and other Arab forces.

What sort of strike caused the government to take emergency steps 'to see the people are fed'?

A dock strike

What was the name of Roy Rogers' horse?

Trigger

Rogers was a hugely popular Hollywood cowboy. He was a special hero of the Saturday matinees. Roy Rogers' Riders Clubs were formed in many cinemas. He was famous for his rodeo skills and Trigger's tricks. Like all the best matinee cowboys, he also sang, on film and record.

Roy Rogers featured in many comic strips as well as toys etc.

Who were the two stars of Spring in Park Lane?

Michael Wilding and Anna Neagle

This English film broke the all-time British box-office record, taking an enormous £1,600,000. It was one of several 'London' films made by Anna Neagle after the war, notable among which was *The Courtneys of Curzon Street* (1947).

Anna Neagle had begun her film career in the 1930s, with starring roles which included Queen Victoria in *Victoria the Great* and nurse Edith Cavell. During the 1940s Anna was voted Britain's top box-office attraction for six consecutive years. In 1950 she gave a fine performance in *Odette*, the true story of a French Resistance heroine. Neagle continued to work during the 1950s, though her films from this period were not as successful.

Which American female singer starred with Gene Kelly in the 1948 musical The Pirate?

Judy Garland

Garland's first major adult part, after her teenage success, had been in *For Me and My Girl* (1942), co-starring with Gene Kelly. Another popular musical came with *Meet Me in St Louis* (1944), in which she sang *The Trolley Song*.

1948 also brought a starring role with Fred Astaire in *Easter Parade*. It was in this film that she sang *We're a Couple of Swells* in a duet with Astaire. Garland's remaining films included *A Star is Born* (1954). Her health was poor throughout her later career. She was troubled by exhaustion, the side-effects of drugs and drink-related problems. Garland died in 1969 after an accidental overdose of sleeping tablets.

What song was sung by Bob Hope, Jane Russell and Roy Rogers in the film The Paleface?

Buttons and Bows

What basic food, which had gone on the ration in 1946, came off in July 1948?

Bread

Bread had not been rationed during the war. However bad harvests in 1945 led to this extension of rationing in the year after the war. Although not rationed, the only type of bread for sale after 1942 was national wholemeal bread. Until then it had still been possible to buy white bread. Shipping losses and the destruction of flour mills then led to all bread being the unpopular wholemeal. Many more women made their bread at home than do today. Home baking provided a valuable opportunity to supplement rations.

What were women now wearing instead of the silk stockings which began to be made again this year?

Nylons

The manufacture of silk stockings in Britain had stopped in 1941. In their absence, rayon, cotton and woollen stockings were substituted, along with socks and leg make-up. By 1948, when silk stockings began to be made again, nylon stockings had come onto the market. Nylons were cheaper, longer-lasting, less shiny and easier to wash than silk stockings, which never regained their popularity.

If you wanted to make a cuppa, what was still in short supply?

Tea, milk and sugar

Tea was first rationed in July 1940 (two ounces per adult per week). By pooling their rations, a family could obtain just enough to use communally. The milk allowance fluctuated. As with many foods, restrictions went on well after the war: the adult allowance in June 1948 was three and a half pints per week (an increase of one pint over the June 1947 ration). The biggest obstacle to the British passion for strong, sweet tea was the sugar shortage. People used honey, treacle, even boiled sweets, in an effort to sweeten their tea. The metallic-tasting saccharine tablet also appeared.

What was a Dickie Suit?

A type of baby clothing

Who started writing her diary at 4 pm on 5 January on the Light Programme?

Mrs Dale in *Mrs Dale's Diary*

This daily radio serial was centred around the everyday life of a doctor's wife and her family. By 1959, 3,000 episodes had been broadcast. (The final episode was broadcast in 1969.) The series title was changed to *The Dales* in 1962. Mrs Dale's GP husband was called Jim; they had a son (Bob) and daughter (Gwen).

Who was christened Charles Philip Arthur George on 15 December?

Prince Charles

Princess Elizabeth's first child had been born on 14 November. The post-war years saw a baby-boom. The birthrate of 1947 had been the highest for 26 years. Many couples were catching up on the lost war years.

Who was the Swedish Hollywood star who featured as Joan of Arc in a film of this year?

Ingrid Bergman

Bergman was a star in Sweden before she came to Hollywood in 1939. During the 1940s, the beautiful new star made several films in America. These included *Casablanca* (1943) with Humphrey Bogart, *For Whom the Bell Tolls* (1943), *The Bells of St Mary's* (1945), *Notorious* (1946) and *Joan of Arc* (1948). Bergman's varied career continued in Europe and Hollywood. She was still appearing in films in the 1970s, winning an Oscar for Best Supporting Actress in *Murder on the Orient Express* (1974).

Who published a book this year which described how he had crossed the Pacific Ocean on a balsa-wood raft named Kon-Tiki?

Thor Heyerdahl

What was taking 895 aircraft flights a day to keep going?

The Berlin airlift

The Soviet Union had blockaded the British, American and French sectors of occupied Berlin in June 1948, as disagreements grew over the future of both the city and Germany. In response the Allies had begun to airlift in the fuel and food needed by the western zones. This was a huge undertaking, with up to 7,000 tons of supplies being flown in each day aboard Dakota transport planes. Bases such as RAF Gatow handled a constant shuttle of aircraft.

The British, American and French zones came together in May to form the new Federal Republic of Germany.

What was the Royal Navy frigate, trapped in the Yangtse river in April by the advancing Chinese?

HMS *Amethyst*

The *Amethyst* was trapped during the advance of Communist Chinese armies on the city of Shanghai. The frigate was shelled and damaged by the Communist forces, several men being killed. In July, the *Amethyst* made a daring 130-mile dash for freedom along the flooded Yangtse river. The frigate was again shelled several times by Chinese batteries and broke through a boom across the river. The crew were later given a hero's welcome when they returned from the East and their acting captain was awarded the DSO.

Who was the world heavyweight champion boxer, known as the Brown Bomber, who hung up his gloves in March?

Joe Louis

Louis had made a record 25 successful defences of his title. His last two title fights had been against Jersey Joe Walcott. The Brown Bomber was now nearly 35 and had begun to slow up when he decided to retire while still at the top. Unfortunately debts and bad advice from hangers-on prompted Louis to come out of retirement in 1951. This comeback ended when the old champion was knocked through the ropes by 28-year-old Rocky Marciano.

What was only worth two dollars eighty cents after it had been devalued by 30 per cent on 18 September?

The pound sterling

Who played all eight members of the d'Ascoyne family in the Ealing Studios comedy Kind Hearts and Coronets?

Alec Guinness

This British comedy tells how a disowned member of a noble family, the d'Ascoynes, plots to murder those relatives who stand between him and the family title. Guinness plays all the members of this eccentric family (both male and female). In 1948, Guinness had made a striking appearance as Fagin in the film of Dickens' novel, *Oliver Twist*.

Which radio series was set on an imaginary RAF station?

Much Binding in the Marsh

This radio comedy series featured Richard Murdoch and Kenneth Horne. It was popular in the late 1940s, with a final series in 1953. At the end of the 1940s, radio was still the most important broadcasting medium.

Which British movie featured the Harry Lime Theme, *played on the zither by Anton Karas?*

The Third Man

This thriller was set in post-war Vienna. Its four stars were Joseph Cotten, Trevor Howard, Orson Welles and Alida Valli. The script was written by Graham Greene. The film's climax comes when Harry Lime (played by Orson Welles) is chased through the Vienna sewers before being shot. When the *Harry Lime Theme* was released on record in 1950 it sold some four million copies.

Which new Christmas character did Gene Autry sing about this year?

Rudolph the Red-nosed Reindeer

Where were more than half of Britain's babies born in the late 1940s?

At home

Home confinements were still common at this time. The creation of the new National Health Service was to encourage hospital births and hospital confinements were to become the more popular practice over the 1950s.

What were switched on in April when a ten-year ban was lifted?

Coloured lights, floodlighting and neon signs

Fuel and power shortages had kept restrictions such as these in force after the war. Rationing was gradually coming to an end. Clothes were taken off 'the ration' in March, sweets and chocolate in April. However Britain's economic struggles led to sweets being rationed again in July. In the same month, the sugar ration fell to eight ounces per week and tobacco supplies were cut.

What expensive, luxury items were housed in veneered wooden cabinets, closed in with doors when not in use, and had 8–12-inch screens?

Television sets

At this time television sets were still a great novelty. Early post-war sets were very expensive in relation to earnings. Table-top models with 8–10-inch screens started at around £50.00. Cabinet models could cost £100.00. Sets operated on several valves, which frequently went wrong. A small, regular television service had been broadcasting since 1936 (though only to the London area). This had been suspended for the duration of the war. In 1949 a transmitter was opened in the Midlands, bringing a greater area of the country into broadcasting range. In 1949 sets were still much-admired status symbols. Fewer than 300,000 homes had sets. Within 10 years, this figure had reached 10 million.

Who were introduced to the second series of Top of the Form *on 3 October?*

Girls

Which North Country comic told stories 'over the garden wall'?

Norman Evans

The act for which Evans is mostly remembered is his impersonation of a toothless housewife who gossiped 'over the garden wall'. During the act, Evans would rest his huge false bosoms on the wall. Popular during the 1940s, Evans made a film, entitled *Over the Garden Wall*, in 1950.

Who opened his Sunday radio show with the cry of 'Wakey, wakey'?

Billy Cotton

This cheerful cockney dance-band leader is best remembered for his *Billy Cotton Band Show*. This consisted of 30 minutes of light music (comedy songs, romantic melodies etc). It was first broadcast in 1949 and ended in 1962, after 500 shows. The series was also to transfer to television, with great success.

Billy Cotton and his band also had one of this year's most popular songs, *I've Got a Lovely Bunch of Coconuts*.

Who made his first appearance on bags of Tate and Lyle sugar this year?

Mr Cube

Tate and Lyle conducted an anti-nationalization campaign in 1949. The Labour government had proposed to take over the sugar industry following the forthcoming election. Mr Cube was part of this campaign, appearing on packets with anti-nationalization slogans.

The Labour government of the time carried out the nationalization (takeover by the State) of several basic industries. These included coal (1947), railways (1948), electricity (1948) and gas (1949). The Bill taking over the iron and steel industry was also introduced this year. These measures created the public corporations, such as The National Coal Board and British Rail, which took over from a collection of private companies.

Who was the busty star of The Outlaw?

Jane Russell

DURING THE early 1950s, Britain was still struggling through the aftermath of the Second World War. The oft-quoted '(You've) never had it so good' would have seemed a little ridiculous to people who had watched their bacon ration fall to three ounces a week during 1950. The housing shortage still meant that many young couples started married life with in-laws or parents, or in tiny flats (usually one or two rooms of a house converted into flats).

While the decade began in this way, the country was to be freed from rationing and restrictions as the 1950s progressed. It was during this time that increasing prosperity set in motion many important changes in people's everyday lives. The character of the 1950s is sometimes distorted by an over-concentration on the start of those trends which were to prove major features of subsequent decades. The 1950s can be best understood as a time which saw the start of many changes but did not experience them for long enough or on a large enough scale to have to deal with their full implications.

Increasing prosperity was reflected in an unprecedented growth in the numbers of washing machines, cookers, refrigerators and television sets (televisions from two million in 1952 to 10 million by the end of the decade). Most of this growth took place after 1955. The weekly cinema audience in 1955 was still 21.2 million, but after the first five years of widely available television it was 9.6 million and falling. Radio also started the decade as an enormously important source of news and entertainment. It entered the 1960s very much in a state of decline, with greatly reduced audiences.

The explosion of private car ownership was just starting at the end of the 1950s. Significantly 1959 saw the release of a revolutionary new model — the mini. At the start of the decade the availability of new cars was very limited and prospective purchasers would often have to go on a waiting list.

The change to Britain as a multiracial society also began in the 1950s. A regular flow of immigrants from Caribbean countries was begun. While the trend had started and there was much press comment on the subject, it should be remembered that the immigrant population was still only approximately a quarter of a million by the end of the decade.

We are often exposed to 1950s nostalgia, which features rock and roll, Bill Haley and Elvis Presley. We tend to forget that in 1952 Vera Lynn had topped the record charts in Britain and America with *Auf Wiedersehen, Sweetheart*. Another movement which began in the 1950s was teenage culture. Popular taste had previously been formed by an older age group. This was another pattern which was established in the 1950s but developed fully in the 1960s. Consideration needs to be given to people whose reputations did not extend much beyond their period of popularity. Alma Cogan, Winifred Atwell and Ruby Murray were 1950s figures who fall into this category.

During the 1950s, crime rates were significantly lower and violence was far less common. However the direction of future behaviour can be seen in its early stages. 'Juvenile delinquency' became a vogue term in some sections of the press.

The 1950s may have seen changes, but they were taking place in a society which was conservative in its attitudes and behaviour. This was a society which did not countenance swearing in the media, found entertainment in Jimmy Clitheroe, operated National Service throughout the decade, had men with short hair and hair cream; which retained strict attitudes to morality and the roles of the sexes, still hanged people, considered Britain to be a great power, had not seen a television advertisement until 1955, had no birth pill and enjoyed ballroom dancing.

What was stolen from Westminster Abbey on Christmas Day?

The Stone of Scone

The Coronation Stone had rested in Westminster Abbey for 650 years, having been taken from Scone in Scotland in 1296 by Edward I. Scottish Nationalists now decided to remove the 458lb 'stone of destiny' from beneath the Coronation Chair and return it to Scotland. It was recovered at Arbroath Abbey in Scotland after a 107-day search.

Where were British soldiers sent to fight in August?

Korea

The Korean war had begun in June, when the Communist North had invaded the South. The United Nations had called for its members to send help to South Korea, but all of the troops which had gone to Korea were American. Britain decided to send forces to assist the Americans in July. The first contingents, composed of men from the Argyll and Sutherland Highlanders and the Middlesex Regiment, arrived in August.

British, Australian and New Zealand troops continued to be involved in the Korean War until its end in 1952, often in the heaviest fighting. The Gloucesters were to make a famous stand at the Imjin river. Despite the presence of these small British contingents, the Korean War was overwhelmingly fought between North Korea and its Chinese backers and South Korea with support from the United States.

Where was the British submarine HMS Truculent involved in a serious accident on 12 January?

The Thames estuary

HMS *Truculent* was on diving trials when it was rammed by a small Swedish vessel. Though only 643 tons, the Swedish ship had been strengthened for ice-breaking, which made the effects of collision worse. A total of 64 seamen were lost in this accident; a few who had been standing on the submarine's conning tower managed to survive. A court martial later blamed the *Truculent*'s captain for hazarding the submarine.

Another submarine was lost in 1951, when HMS *Affray* went missing off the south coast. This was a mysterious incident in which there were no survivors from the *Affray*'s crew of 75. After investigation, the disappearance was blamed on the *Affray*'s faulty breathing equipment.

Which party won the February General Election, with an overall majority of only three seats?

Labour

Which American star made his London debut in July, having just ousted Bing Crosby as the highest-paid singer in the United States?

Frank Sinatra

Sinatra came to the London Palladium and was besieged by his young, mostly female fans. He had only previously been seen in England in films such as *On the Town* (1949) with Gene Kelly. He had begun his career with the Tommy Dorsey Band and remained a top performer for many years. His later records were to include the well-known *Strangers in the Night* and *My Way* (1966).

Who knocked England's football team out of the World Cup in 1950? (The winning goal was scored by their unheard of centre forward, Larry Gaetjens.)

The United States of America (1–0)

England had gone to Brazil, for the fourth World Cup, as joint favourites to win the trophy. They had won their opening match against Chile 2–0. Their next game was with the footballing unknowns of the United States. The American team was a collection of multinational immigrants with hardly any experience of international football. The English team boasted its usual line-up of stars, including Tom Finney and Billy Wright. To everyone's amazement the Americans scored just before half-time and England made a very sad exit from their first World Cup.

What was unusual about James Stewart's friend Harvey in the film of the same name?

He was an invisible six-foot tall white rabbit

In this film Stewart repeated his stage role as the eccentric Elwood P Dowd. Stewart had made a number of successful films before the war (such as *Mr Smith Goes to Washington* in 1939), but was having difficulty in renewing his screen career after the war. He eventually made a deal with Universal Studios which gave him a percentage of his films' profits, dependent on his making them for a lower salary. This was an unusual agreement at the time and obviously depended on his post-war films being popular. Fortunately for Stewart, the movies made under the agreement did prove popular, especially the Western *Winchester 73* (1950) and *The Glenn Miller Story* (1954) in which he played the bandleader.

Which singer had a big hit this year with Mona Lisa?

Nat King Cole

What was the Minister of Health warning smugglers to stop bringing across the Irish Sea in an announcement this January?

Canned and dried fruit, table jellies, chocolate and confectionery

Britain was still having to endure rationing and shortages. (This was five years after the end of the war.) Dr Edith Summerskill was the Labour government's Minister of Health who issued these warnings.

What new radio programme was introduced with the words "Are you sitting comfortably? Then I'll begin"?

Listen with Mother

This was a daily 15 minutes of simple songs, nursery rhymes and stories provided for children under five. The famous introduction was first heard in 1950 and the final programme was in 1982.

Which much-sequined leisure activity featured on a new television programme this year?

Ballroom dancing (on *Come Dancing*)

The 1950s saw a boom in ballroom dancing. The standard four dances — waltz, foxtrot, quickstep and tango — combined with eight-couple 'formation' dancing to provide entertainment on the new BBC programme *Come Dancing*. An equal attraction for many was the dresses of the dancers. These were usually made up of yards of net in many layers, encased in a sequined overlay. The interest in ballroom dancing led to the international championship being established at the Albert Hall in 1953.

What new fabric did ICI announce that it was going to make in its new factory at Redcar?

Terylene

What colour was Maureen O'Hara's hair?

Red

O'Hara was a Universal-International star of the 1940s and 1950s. She had appeared in the Oscar-winning *How Green Was My Valley* earlier on in her career (1941). After the war she featured in a number of average-quality films such as *Baghdad* (1949) and *Flame of Araby* (1951). In 1950 she starred in a Western, *Comanche Territory*. If nothing else, these films showed off her colouring in glorious Technicolor.

What are the best-known words spoken by Robert Newton in this year's Walt Disney version of Treasure Island?

"Aha, Jim lad"

This was an important film for Walt Disney as it was his first all-live action feature. Disney was in financial difficulties at the time and badly needed some box-office success which did not incur the enormous production costs of his feature-length cartoon films. He achieved this with a splendid adaptation of Robert Louis Stevenson's pirate tale. Robert Newton provided the highlight of the film with his memorable portrayal of Long John Silver.

What was PC Archibald-Willoughby's number in a radio series of this time?

PC 49

The Adventures of PC 49 was first heard in 1947 and last broadcast in 1953. The way in which the police are depicted in popular drama can provide an indicator of the way the Force has changed. PC 49 is a long way from DI Burnside in *The Bill*. At the beginning of the 1950s, car ownership was not widespread enough to change the large-scale use of the foot patrol. As car-related theft and traffic control were not the enormous problems of today, the Bobby on the beat was still a familiar sight. Violence against the police was rare and regarded very seriously. The police were under a lot less pressure. Some areas of crime, such as drugs and drug-related offences, were hardly known of. In the days before the aerosol can there was not even a lot of vandalism.

Which American tennis player made the news because of the frilly white panties she wore at Wimbledon this year?

Gussy Moran

What Exhibition did the King open in London on 3 May?

The Festival of Britain

This was a government-sponsored event which aimed to provide some fantasy and colour for a hard-pressed Britain. The architecture of the exhibition included the Dome of Discovery and the tall, thin, aluminium Skylon. One lasting feature of the Festival was the Royal Festival Hall on the south bank of the Thames. There were also Festival pleasure gardens at Battersea Park. The Exhibition cost over £8 million, an expense which was heavily criticized by Conservatives and the newspapers.

Where was the Emergency?

Malaya

The Emergency was the term used for the guerilla war fought against Communist insurgents in Malaya. The guerillas drew support from the ethnic Chinese groups settled in that country. The problems of how to deal with this violent conflict occupied the British government over the first half of the decade. British troops fought alongside Malayan police against the insurgents. By 1951 the Communists had become more selective in their targets. In this year, the High Commissioner, Sir Ivor Gurney, was killed. The Emergency was brought under control through a range of measures which included the resettlement of Chinese sympathisers as well as direct police operations. Malaya became independent in 1957.

Which two British diplomats went missing in May?

Guy Burgess and Donald MacLean

Burgess and Maclean were products of Eton and Oxbridge. Despite their Establishment background they had been recruited as Soviet agents in the 1930s. This meant that they could act as Soviet double agents when they went on to serve in sensitive Foreign Office and diplomatic service posts. They made a joint defection in May and fled to Moscow, having been warned of their impending discovery by a fellow double agent. The Foreign Office did not admit to Burgess and Maclean having been Soviet agents until 1955. The Third Man in this episode was named (in 1955) as Kim Philby.

How many of the 36 starters finished this year's Grand National?

Three (Nickel Coin was the winner)

In what television game did the panel have to discover the jobs of invited guests, using only 10 questions?

What's my Line?

This programme was launched by the BBC in 1951 with Eamonn Andrews in the chair. Panellists included Gilbert Harding and Lady Isobel Barnett. The game was based on an earlier radio show, *Twenty Questions*. *What's my Line?* ended a 12-year run in 1963, with an audience of 10 million.

Who was the star of The Cruel Sea?

Jack Hawkins

This screen adaptation of the famous novel by Nicholas Monsarrat was among the most popular films of the year in Britain. Jack Hawkins played the captain of the *Compass Rose*. Like most British films of the time it was cheaply made when compared to Hollywood movies.

Which stage musical opened on Broadway this year and featured the song Shall We Dance?

The King and I

This Rodgers and Hammerstein musical was a great stage success as well as being made into a very popular film musical in 1956. It tells the story of the relationship between the King of Siam and the English governess he employs to look after his many royal children. Yul Brynner played the role of the king, both on stage and in the film. The governess in the film was Deborah Kerr. The show also featured the popular *Hello Young Lovers*.

Who was the singing star who featured in this year's film The Great Caruso?

Mario Lanza

What title was Kiki Haakonson the first to win?

Miss World

This annual beauty contest to find the world's most glamorous woman was launched in 1951. The event was sponsored by Eric Morley's Mecca empire. Miss Sweden was the first to win the crown. It was to be 10 years before the United Kingdom contestant would win (Rosemarie Frankland, in 1961).

Why were small squares of cloth made to drape over the top of armchair backs?

To protect them from men's haircream

During the 1950s, men's hairstyles were still generally restricted to short back and sides. The first signs of long hair came later in the decade, when a small number of Teddy Boys grew their hair a little. However even this was frowned upon and long hair for men was not going to arrive until the 1960s.

Sales of *Brylcreem* and *Silvikrin* were also much greater in the 1950s, as it was still common practice for men of all ages to grease down their hair. The use of haircream was to decrease during the decade, but the product was to be worse hit in the 1960s by the advent of long hair.

What was just beginning to revolutionize people's writing habits?

The ball-point pen

The *Biro* had been invented by a Hungarian journalist named Ladislas Biro. He had sold out to an English backer, HG Martin, who began to market the new pens in the years just after the war. The *Biro* is now so common that it is difficult to imagine a time without it. In the early 1950s these pens were still very much an innovation, though they would quickly become more common. Many traditionalists complained that they made people's handwriting messier.

What did the 1951 census show that one in three households did not have?

A fixed bath

Who was the youngest Conservative candidate in this year's General Election?

Margaret Hilda Roberts (Mrs Thatcher)

Britain's Prime Minister for the 1980s was only 26 in 1951. She failed to win the Dartford seat in this election, but was back in 1959 to become the MP for Finchley. Shortly after her 1951 defeat, Margaret Roberts had married Dennis, to become Mrs Thatcher. She was the Conservative's youngest MP in 1959 and gained minor government experience in 1961. However Mrs Thatcher was to spend most of the 1960s as an Opposition spokeswoman. Her first major ministerial job came in 1970 — as Minister of Education in Edward Heath's new government.

Who was the young Leamington boxer who became world middleweight champion this year?

Randolph Turpin

Turpin came from a boxing family. His brother Dick had broken a colour bar to become the first black boxer to take the Commonwealth and British titles in 1948. Brother Jackie was also a passable featherweight. The youngest brother, Randolph had the most spectacular career. Within a nine-month period, Randolph won the British and Commonwealth crowns once held by his brother, then went on to become the world champion. His opponent in this title fight was Sugar Ray Robinson.

Turpin was to lose a second meeting with Robinson, but at only 23 he had seven more years of successful boxing to come (though mixed with an occasional setback). Randolph Turpin retired as British champion in 1958 and his boxing career faded during the early 1960s. He was disturbed that he had virtually nothing to show for all the money earned by his spectacular career in the ring. In 1966 he took his own life, aged 37.

Which comedian had the catch-phrase "You Lucky People"?

Tommy Trinder

Trinder was a cockney comic who had a long career in radio and television. He appeared in many shows, the first weekly series being *Tommy Trinder Goes Job Hunting*. This was sponsored by Symington's table creams on Radio Luxembourg from 15 May 1938. Other radio shows included *Tommy Get Your Fun* – half an hour of comedy for 'You Lucky People'. This show also featured Claude Hulbert and Dorothy Carless. His show *The Trinder Box* was first broadcast on 1 October 1951.

Which famous American general did President Truman sack as the commander of United Nations forces in Korea on 11 April?

General Douglas MacArthur

What was the secret society responsible for the increasing violent unrest in Kenya?

The Mau Mau

Kenya was another trouble spot in which British soldiers filled a policing role during the 1950s. There was a state of emergency there from 1952 to 1959, as the Mau Mau carried out a campaign of terror against their European rulers. Stories about gruesome Mau Mau initiation ceremonies were not solely press exaggeration, and the acts of violence carried out in the troubles were particularly gruesome.

A suspected leader of the Mau Mau, Jomo Kenyatta, was imprisoned for much of the 1950s but was to become the country's first Premier when it gained independence in 1963.

What did BOAC's Comet become when it entered scheduled service on 2 May?

The world's first jet airliner

British designers had taken advantage of their lead in jet propulsion to work on the Comet. When the new airliner entered service, orders were coming in from airlines all over the world.

Unfortunately BOAC were to lose this lead when problems began to appear in their pioneering aircraft. When three Comets were lost after breaking up, the Comet was grounded while investigations were carried out on the jet which had crashed into the sea near Elba. These showed that the fuselage had weakened and broken up because of its repeated pressurizing and depressurizing. By the time this fault had been corrected, other countries had caught up with BOAC and were producing their own jet airliners (having also gained from BOAC's painful lessons).

What sort of fish made the news this year when it was caught off Madagascar?

A coelacanth

This fish was believed to have been extinct for 50 million years. Professor JBL Smith had suspected that this might not be the case since he had heard reports of an earlier catch in 1938, when he had leaflets printed and distributed in the likely areas for another catch. These did not have any result until 14 years later when someone familiar with the leaflet rescued a coelacanth from a fish market. This long-lost creature was 5 ft long and weighed 100 lb.

What horse helped win Britain's only gold medal at this year's Helsinki Olympics?

Foxhunter

Who was Singin' in the Rain *this year?*

Gene Kelly

Kelly was one of the biggest musical stars of the 1940s and early 1950s. *Singin' in the Rain* was one of his most popular films. It includes the classic scene where he dances through a rainstorm singing the title-song. Kelly's pleasant voice and dancing talents had also featured in *For Me and My Girl* (1942), opposite Judy Garland, *Cover Girl* (1944), with Rita Hayworth, and *An American in Paris* (1951).

Which radio situation comedy series starred the husband and wife team of Ben Lyon and Bebe Daniels, together with their real-life children Barbara and Richard?

Life with the Lyons

This husband and wife team had been Hollywood stars. With their careers on the wane they found success in Britain, notably in radio. The first series of *Life with the Lyons* was broadcast in 1950, the last in 1961. Their wartime series *Hi Gang* (1940 to 1942) was also a great hit.

Who began her radio shows with Yours *and closed with* Auf Wiedersehen, Sweetheart?

Vera Lynn

Vera Lynn was still a big star in the early 1950s as well as being popular during the war years. Her radio shows *Vera Lynn Sings* were recorded before a different services audience each week and broadcast by Radio Luxembourg — 'Songs for forces everywhere, their wives and sweethearts, their families and friends'. Vera began the series at RAF Stanmore, sponsored by *Horlicks*. In the next series the sponsors were *Kraft Cheese*. Vera also went into television in the 1950s with her own show.

Which team won the FA Cup for the second year running when they defeated Arsenal 1–0 on 3 May?

Newcastle United (captained by Joe Harvey)

What small folding card was finally abolished this year?

The identity card

These cards were a hangover from wartime. They had been introduced at the beginning of the war and by law everyone was supposed to carry one and produce it on demand. By now they had become an irrelevance and a minor act of the new Conservative government was to abolish them. Though gone, they were not to be quite forgotten as, for convenience, the number from a person's identity card was converted into their new health service number.

What was to take the place of enamel bowls in the kitchen during the 1950s?

Coloured plastic

Plastics brought a revolution in people's everyday lives, especially in the kitchen. It is sometimes difficult to imagine a pre-plastic time. Wooden plate racks, enamel bowls, wicker laundry baskets — all these were replaced by coloured, flexible and washable plastic utensils.

What great British habit was freed from rationing on 3 October?

Tea drinking

The early 1950s saw the end of the remaining rationing, though many goods were still in short supply. Luxury goods were especially restricted, as they were more likely to be sent for export. The year 1952 also saw an increase in the meat ration to 1/7d per week. The cheese ration, though, had fallen to an ounce a week in April.

Another sign of the ending of wartime controls was the termination of the Utility Scheme in March. The British Standards kite mark replaced the Utility sign.

What new footwear fashion made young women look taller?

Stiletto heels

Who was Christopher Craig's partner in crime?

Derek Bentley

Craig and Bentley were involved in the shooting of a London police constable on the roof of a warehouse. They had been discovered during a bungled robbery. Craig had actually fired the shots but he escaped the death penalty because of his youth (he was 16). Bentley was sentenced to hang after the court heard a police witness describe how Bentley had shouted "Let him have it, Chris" to Craig. Bentley claimed to have meant the gun itself.

Who was being educated on a well-known radio comedy programme of the 1950s?

Archie in *Educating Archie*

Archie Andrews was a ventriloquist's dummy. Although there were a number of human characters in the series, the most important figure was always Archie (the ventriloquist being Peter Brough). Several series were broadcast between 1950 and 1960.

As who was Leslie Welch better known? He often answered questions with "I think I'm right in saying . . ."?

The Memory Man

In 1947 *Beat the Memory Man* was a regular feature in *Navy Mixture* and later Welch had a similar spot in *Calling All Forces*. In 1952 he featured in a Radio Luxembourg series, *Beat the Memory Man*, sponsored by *Bovril*. Listeners received a guinea for every question correctly answered or £25 if they stumped him.

What sort of sportswoman was 17-year-old Maureen Connolly (Little Mo)?

A tennis player (she was the Wimbledon champion in 1952)

What very unpleasant condition began to affect Britain's rabbits this year?

Myxomatosis

This virus was spread deliberately by farmers. They argued that it was necessary because rabbits caused millions of pounds' worth of damage to crops each year. Myxomatosis almost wiped out the rabbit population in some counties, the animals dying in a painful and unpleasant way.

Who was the infamous resident of 10 Rillington Place, Notting Hill, who came to trial this year?

John Reginald Halliday Christie

Christie was arrested on 31 March after a large police manhunt, launched after the new tenant of Christie's house had discovered the remains of three women walled up in the recently vacated building. Christie had murdered these three women, as well as his wife, whose body was under the floorboards.

Christie was to be hanged on 15 July, having confessed to three further killings. These victims included Mrs Beryl Evans and her small daughter. Three years before, Christie had been the chief prosecution witness at the trial of Timothy John Evans, who had lived with his wife at Rillington Place. On Christie's evidence he was found guilty of her murder and hanged. It was not until October 1966 that Evans was granted a free pardon by the Queen.

What caused large amounts of damage and loss of life in East Anglia at the end of January?

Serious flooding

On 31 January, the North Sea overcame several of East Anglia's sea defences as the result of some of the worst weather conditions this century. Winds of 113 mph were recorded in Scotland. In the lowland regions of England there was no time for warnings to save cattle or, more seriously, people. The death toll of 307 included 17 Americans on the US Air Force base at Hunstanton.

The River Ouse was forced back up its course and rose a record 31 feet. Thousands were made temporarily homeless as flooding affected villages up to five miles inland. Lincolnshire and Essex were also badly affected.

What was the name of the car ferry which sank in the Irish Sea in January, with the loss of 128 lives?

The Princess Victoria

What did Danny Kaye's 'ugly duckling' turn into?

A swan

Kaye sang this song in the musical *Hans Christian Andersen* (1953) which also featured *The King's New Clothes*. Danny Kaye was one of Hollywood's biggest musical-comedy stars in the late 1940s. His films included *Wonder Man* (with Virginia Mayo, 1945) and *The Secret Life of Walter Mitty* (1947). By the time he made *The Court Jester* in 1955 he was past his most popular period. A feature of Kaye's musicals was his singing of novelty 'tongue-twisters' such as *Gilly Gilly Ossenfeffer Katzenellen Bogen by the Sea*.

What was the score when England played Hungary at Wembley in November?

England lost 3–6

Hungary became the first overseas national team to defeat England at Wembley. England's tactics were rather old-fashioned compared to those of the East Europeans. Hungary became one of the great international sides of the 1950s. Their captain was Ferenc Puskas, who scored two of their goals in this game. The Hungarian centre-forward, Hidekguti, completed a hat-trick.

For which television variety show did the theatre audience have to wear costume as well as the performers?

The Good Old Days

Chaired by Leonard Sachs, this show was broadcast from the City Varieties Theatre, Leeds. It took the form of a night at the music-hall, where the audience dressed up in bonnets and shawls, boaters and blazers. It was first shown by the BBC in 1953.

Which well-known Western featured Gary Cooper as the lone hero and a song by Tex Ritter?

High Noon

What was the first national, branded, sliced loaf?

Wonderloaf

The 1950s saw the introduction of many types of convenience food. The branded sliced loaf was one of these new developments. New types of food were appearing as a new way of shopping was beginning to be seen. In 1950 Sainsbury's first self-service store had opened in Croydon. These were only the first steps in the change-over, but it was to be a process which would be followed by the majority of large shops over the 1950s and 1960s.

What was the cheapest small family car available in this year?

The Ford Popular — £390 (including purchase tax)

A price war had developed in the small family car market. In 1953 the Popular was the cheapest four-cylinder car available. Its competitors included Austin's two-door version of the A30 — £475 (on the road) and the four-door Standard Eight — at £481.

What were beginning to enjoy a new popularity on the breakfast table?

Breakfast cereals

Cereals, such as *Force*, had been available previously, but popularity grew with the availability of more brands to choose from (*Shredded Wheat* and *Puffed Wheat* are examples). As with tea-drinking, a larger number of people preferred a more traditional start to the day, with bacon, egg and sausage.

What returned to the petrol pumps this year?

Branded petrol

Who stood on the peak of Mount Everest on 29 May?

New Zealander Edmund Hilary and Nepalese Sherpa Tensing

Hilary and Tensing were the first men to reach the peak of the highest mountain in the world. They were part of a British expedition led by Colonel John Hunt. Though they reached the peak on 29 May, the story broke on the following day.

Which popular singer/movie star appeared as Calamity Jane this year?

Doris Day

Day began as a singer with the hit record *Sentimental Journey* before she came to the movies. Nearly all of her films were eager-to-please escapism. One of the best remembered is *Calamity Jane*, which co-starred Howard Keel. Songs such as *Secret Love*, *The Deadwood Stage* and *The Black Hills of Dakota* made it a box-office hit. Day made a series of popular comedies in the late 1950s and early 1960s. These included *Teacher's Pet* (1958), with a hit title song, *Pillow Talk*, with Rock Hudson (1959), *Please Don't Eat the Daisies*, with David Niven (1960) and *The Glass Bottom Boat*, with Rod Taylor (1966). At the end of the 1960s she went into US television. Day left showbusiness altogether in 1974.

To many, Doris Day was the ultimate girl-next-door. This together with songs such as *Que Sera Sera (Whatever will be, will be)* and *Move Over Darling* made her enormously popular.

Who was the 38-year-old hero of the Blackpool–Bolton Wanderers FA Cup Final?

Stanley Matthews

The veteran right winger had not won an FA cup-winner's medal during his career. In the 1952/53 season, he was to get a chance to add a winner's medal to his other honours when Blackpool met Bolton Wanderers at Wembley. In the Matthews Final he made two goals as Blackpool came from 3–1 behind to win 4–3. Blackpool scored their winner with only a minute left to play. Stan Mortensen played centre-forward for Blackpool in the final.

Who did 25 million people watch on 2 June, in a ceremony never before televised?

Queen Elizabeth II (during the Coronation)

What did Roger Bannister become the first man to do in less than four minutes?

Run the mile

A 25-year-old medical student, Bannister broke the four-minute barrier on 6 May at the university track at Oxford. His pace-setters had been Chris Chataway and Chris Brasher. Running the last lap in 59 seconds, Bannister broke the tape in 3 minutes 59.4 seconds.

Where were French troops defeated in a siege this year?

Dien Bien Phu

France had been the controlling power in Vietnam before the war. During the war they had been displaced by a Japanese occupation. They now became involved in a conflict with the Vietnamese Communists in an attempt to re-establish their position in Vietnam. This fighting came to a climax with the siege of Dien Bien Phu. 12,000 French troops (mainly Vietnamese and Colonial French legionnaires) had dug into this position and confidently awaited attack by the Communist forces. They believed that the Vietminh would not be able to transport artillery through the difficult jungle terrain; the French also had a strong advantage in aircraft. However they received a shock when the Communists brought in artillery by carrying dismantled guns on bicycles, then reassembling them around the French position. This meant that the Communists were able to keep up a heavy bombardment of the French force. The French fought back strongly, but the end came at the beginning of May, when they were overwhelmed by the Communist forces.

What did Parliament present to Sir Winston Churchill on his eightieth birthday?

A portrait by Graham Sutherland

In a ceremony recorded by television, Clement Attlee presented the painting to Churchill. Sutherland was known for his marked lack of flattery in portrait painting. In his acceptance speech, Sir Winston showed a noticeable lack of enthusiasm when he described the portrait as 'certainly combining force with candour'.

The painting was discreetly hidden from Churchill's view, but even the knowledge of its existence played on his mind. Following Lady Churchill's death in 1978 it was revealed that it had been burned within a couple of years of being painted.

What disease was the Salk vaccine (now undergoing independent trials) supposed to prevent?

Polio

Who did seven brothers meet up with in a successful 1954 musical?

Seven brides

Seven Brides for Seven Brothers was an unexpected hit for the studio which made it (MGM). The film starred Howard Keel and Jane Powell. It was not made on an enormous budget, as can be seen from the rather obvious backdrop used in much of the movie. The film succeeds in overcoming such flaws through the strength of its songs and energetic choreography. The small, blonde Powell had been a surprising choice to many people but her clear soprano voice proved eminently suitable for songs such as *When You're in Love*.

What film set just before the bombing of Pearl Harbor swept the Oscars this year?

From Here to Eternity

Based on a popular novel by James Jones, this movie followed the lives of a group of soldiers serving in Hawaii just before Pearl Harbor was attacked. It starred Burt Lancaster, Deborah Kerr (in an untypical role) and Frank Sinatra. The film includes the well-known scene with Burt Lancaster and Deborah Kerr on the beach while the waves wash over them. The book had been considered quite daring at the time and the film was also thought quite adult. It won eight Oscars in all.

Who was Jerry Lewis's singing comedy partner?

Dean Martin

Martin and Lewis were a comic duo on film for the first half of the 1950s. They had worked together on stage before this but their first film together was in 1950. In their films, Martin was the good-looking, easy-going crooner, while Lewis played an awkward, accident-prone young man. They made 14 films together between 1950 and 1956, before going their separate ways. Lewis went on to make over 20 solo comedy films, while Martin became a successful singer, actor and television performer.

Which British singer had a runaway success with her record Softly Softly?

Ruby Murray

What flashing lights began to show the way from January?

Flashing direction indicators on motor vehicles

Before flashing indicators, cars had small mechanical arms which were fixed to its sides. These were raised in the direction the car was to turn at the appropriate moment. Before these, hand-signals were used. New cars on the market now featured flashing indicators. These models also featured more design extras, such as more trim and more streamlining.

What brand became Nescafe's first real competitor in the instant coffee market this year?

Maxwell House

As in many areas, eating and drinking habits show the beginnings of change in the 1950s, without actually experiencing those changes in a major way. While it might have become fashionable for some younger people to drink in coffee bars, Britain was to remain overwhelmingly a tea-drinking nation during the decade. In 1958, market research indicated that, at breakfast, 85 per cent of the population drank tea and 4 per cent drank coffee.

What inspection were motorists told they would have to worry about in the near future?

MOT tests

The Road Traffic Bill of 1954 announced that regular, compulsory inspections of motor vehicles were to be introduced. These became known as MOT tests (from Ministry of Transport). This meant that, once a year, car-owners would have to prove their vehicles were safe and roadworthy. Tests were put into effect at the end of the decade.

What did the old age pension go up to in 1954?

£2 per week (single)

Who was the American evangelist who preached to a Wembley crowd of over 120,000 on 22 May?

Billy Graham

Graham came to England and preached for 72 consecutive nights in his Greater London Crusade of 1954. He then travelled round other parts of the country, speaking to nearly three million people in total. The Wembley meeting was the climax of his London crusade and the huge crowd was assembled despite the pouring rain. At the same time that Billy Graham was attracting this interest, church attendances were falling and interest in conventional religious worship was declining.

Which jockey became the youngest ever winner of the Derby in this year?

Lester Piggot

The 18-year-old Piggot rode the 33–1 outsider Never Say Die to this Derby win. He was to ride 4,349 winners by the time of his retirement from the saddle in 1985. During his career, he was champion jockey 11 times. Lester Piggot was to ride some great horses over his long career, the best of all being Nijinsky, from 1969.

After his retirement, Piggot made news again when he was sentenced to a three-year prison term for tax evasion. He was to serve 12 months, before his release in 1988.

Which woman singer couldn't tell a waltz from a tango in 1954?

Alma Cogan

This 1950s singer was famous for her vivacious personality and large wardrobe of gowns. She had featured in the radio series, *Take It From Here* (1953 to 1954). Alma Cogan was consistently popular, with UK chart hits *Bell Bottom Blues, Little Things Mean a Lot* and *I Can't Tell a Waltz from a Tango* (all in 1954). She had a number one in 1955, with *Dreamboat*. Later, from 1959 to 1961, she had her own television show on ITV.

Who was Bolton Wanderers' and England's bustling centre-forward?

Nat Lofthouse

Who succeeded Winston Churchill as Tory Prime Minister in April?

Sir Anthony Eden

At 80 and also increasingly frail, Churchill resigned the premiership on 5 April. He remained in the Commons as a backbencher. Eden had long been his expected successor. Only 16 days after becoming Prime Minister he called for a General Election, which he and the Conservatives were to win handsomely, with a majority of 58. This was the first time for nearly 100 years that the party in office had appealed for a fresh mandate and received an increased majority.

Who was the last woman to hang?

Ruth Ellis

Ellis, a platinum blonde ex-model, was found guilty of murder on 21 June. She had shot her lover, racing driver David Blakely, outside a pub in Hampstead. Blakely had died from two wounds in the back from a revolver. Shortly before this, Ellis had been begging him not to leave her. Ruth Ellis was hanged at Holloway Prison on 13 July. She was aged 28.

Who became the new leader of the Labour Party after Mr Attlee?

Hugh Gaitskell

At 49, Gaitskell was young for a party leader. He had defeated the veteran Herbert Morrison and left-wing Aneurin Bevan by clear majorities. Gaitskell was to lead the party through the 1950s and into the early 1960s. However his moderate approach was never to be tested in power, as he died after a short illness in 1963.

Who was the young star of Rebel Without a Cause *and* East of Eden *who died in a car crash on 30 September?*

James Dean

What game show featured Box 13 and the Yes/No sequence?

Take Your Pick

This show made its debut on ITV's first week in 1955. It was hosted by Michael Miles for nearly 20 years. Contestants first had to endure the Yes/No sequence, where they had to answer a barrage of questions without using the words 'yes' or 'no'. They then had to answer three questions for the opportunity to collect a key to one of the ten boxes, which contained a variety of prizes (three were booby prizes and one was the mystery box 13). Miles would then try to buy the key off the player and the audience were noisy in their advice to 'open the box' or 'take the money' (usually about £10–£20). When a winner got to open a box they could find it contained anything from a star prize to a dried prune. *Take Your Pick* had originally been a Radio Luxembourg programme.

Which well-known farewell did PC George Dixon come out with each week?

'Evenin' All'

Dixon of Dock Green was a long-running television series which began in 1955 and continued for 21 years through 367 episodes. The series had originally been based on the cinema film *The Blue Lamp*, in which Jack Warner had also starred. He then took the role of PC George Dixon in the television series (Sergeant Dixon in the later years of the programme).

Which American singer had a big hit this year with his version of Ain't That a Shame?

Pat Boone

Boone's success was built on his clean-cut image. At the time, this made him the second most popular singer to Elvis Presley. Many of his hits were covers of songs by black artists (as with Fats Waller's *Ain't That a Shame*). His most popular records were sentimental ballads, such as *Love Letters in the Sand* (1957) and *April Love* (1957). His last chart entry was in 1961, with the novelty *Speedy Gonzales*.

Boone claimed to be a direct descendant of frontiersman Daniel Boone and was noted for wearing white bucks (shoes).

Who sang He's a Tramp *in the Walt Disney film* The Lady and the Tramp?

Peggy Lee

What was the first ever British television commercial for?

Gibbs SR toothpaste

This was shown on the first night of independent television (22 September 1955). A number of public figures were vocal opponents of commercial television. Some were afraid of the way adverts would affect the quality of the programmes, others (such as newspapers) were simply wary of the competition for advertisers.

Why were people wearing glasses with red and green lenses?

To watch 3D films

The audience of a 3D (three-dimensional) film was supplied with special glasses to view the film. These glasses had one red and one green lens. 3D was a gimmick used for a short while in an effort to win back audiences from television. Cinema attendances had fallen drastically. Technical innovations such as CinemaScope (wide-screen films) also had little effect on the decline in audience figures. As a result, many cinemas were closing. Rank shut down 91 between 1956 and 1959.

Who brought out Britain's first frozen fish fingers this year?

Bird's Eye

The 1950s saw the arrival of convenience foods, sliced bread, instant coffee and fish fingers. The availability of frozen goods reflects the increasing incidence of electrical appliances. More people now had a refrigerator. Compared to today, many of the cookers and other appliances appear very bulky and badly de-signed. Yet it is important to remember that what appears a museum piece to us was advertised at the time as the latest in kitchen technology. It is interesting to consider how different everyday life was, when sliced bread and fish fingers were consi-dered innovations.

What was distinctive about the 16 young men arrested for fighting outside a Bath dance-hall on 28 May?

They were Teddy Boys

Who died in a fire in Ambridge on 22 September?

Grace Archer in the radio serial *The Archers*

This radio series began regular broadcasts on the Light Programme in 1951. *The Archers* was, and still is, based on the life of a farming family who live at Brookfield Farm in Ambridge (a village dreamt up by the serial's writers). On the evening of 22 September 1955, the BBC distracted much attention from ITV's opening night by killing Grace Archer in a fire.

The serial goes on today, though with many cast and character changes. Original characters included Dan and Doris Archer, their children Philip, Jack and Christine and neighbour Walter Gabriel.

Who hosted the popular television game show Double Your Money?

Hughie Green

Hughie ("and I mean this sincerely, folks") Green was a regular question-master on this show for nearly 20 years. Contestants were asked a series of questions on a subject of their choice and the prize money doubled up each time they answered correctly, starting at £1 and going up to £32.

There was then a chance to go for a £1,000 jackpot. If the player could answer a test question they would go into the 'box' where the questions would get tougher. Prize money now 'doubled up' to £64, £125, £250, £500 and finally £1,000. A contestant could 'stick' at any point and take the corresponding amount (these were significant sums at the time). If they went on and got a question wrong, they lost everything. Green's assistant was Monica Rose, a one-time player who proved so popular she was invited back to introduce the contestants.

Who did Princess Margaret announce that she would not *marry in October?*

Group Captain Peter Townsend

Pressure was brought upon the Princess because the group captain was the innocent party in a divorce. Attitudes to divorce were still fairly conservative. If the Princess had married Townsend, she would have lost her place as third in line to the throne and would also have had to give up her payments from the Civil List. Any marriage would have had to be a civil ceremony because of the Church's attitude to divorce (although by 1957 the Church of England was to declare that remarried divorcees could take the sacraments if a Bishop permitted). The episode provided a big newspaper story at the time.

Who was the woman star of the first imported American situation comedy series shown on television?

Lucille Ball (in *I Love Lucy*)

Where were British and French soldiers sent on a joint operation early in November?

Suez

This incident had originated in the Egyptian seizure of the Suez Canal in July. Colonel Nasser had then announced that he was nationalizing the Anglo-French-controlled Suez Canal Company. After international attempts to find a solution had failed, the French and British took the situation into their own hands through military intervention. The Canal Zone was occupied and bombing raids were made on Egyptian airfields. A cease-fire was imposed by the United Nations after eight days. The United States was strongly opposed to the Anglo-French action and it was American financial pressure which forced a withdrawal from Suez, beginning at the end of November.

Who did the American playwright, Arthur Miller, marry in 1956?

Marilyn Monroe

Born Norma Jean Baker, her first important film was *The Asphalt Jungle* (1950). After a number of early films came parts in *Niagara* (1952) and *Gentlemen prefer Blondes* (1953), with Jane Russell. In this, Marilyn sang *Diamonds Are a Girl's Best Friend*. Monroe's best remembered films are mostly musical comedies. *How to Marry a Millionaire* (1953) also featured Betty Grable and Lauren Bacall.

In 1954 she married Joe DiMaggio, a famous baseball player. She divorced him in 1955, the year of *The Seven-Year Itch*. Marilyn now tried to get herself accepted as a more serious actress. *Bus Stop* (1956) dates from this period. She returned to comedy for *Some Like It Hot* (1959), co-starring Jack Lemmon and Tony Curtis. The last film she completed was *The Misfits* (1961). In 1962 Marilyn Monroe overdosed in a 'probable suicide'. She was 36.

Which city were Soviet tanks sent into at the start of November?

Budapest

During 1956 Hungary had seen an uprising against Soviet rule. This had brought Imre Nagy into power as Prime Minister. He promised to begin negotiations for the removal of Soviet troops and for democratization. The Soviets did withdraw their troops while they assessed the situation. When the Hungarian revolt continued and its objectives became more threatening to the Soviets, Moscow decided to quash it. In early November, 1,000 tanks entered Budapest. The Russian force suppressed the rebellion and a new pro-Soviet government was formed. Nagy was eventually hanged in 1958.

Which two Soviet leaders visited London in April?

Nikita Khrushchev and Nikolai Bulganin

What famous talent show did Hughie Green present on both radio and television?

Opportunity Knocks

This talent-spotting show was a radio favourite for several years. From 1950 it was broadcast from Radio Luxembourg, sponsored by *Horlicks*. It became the longest-running television talent show. The first transmission was in 1956 and the last in 1977, still hosted by Hughie Green, now famous for his catch-phrase, "and I mean this sincerely, folks". The contestants on television were judged by the Clappometer, which responded to the studio audience's applause for an act, plus the viewers' votes.

Who was the British singer with the skiffle hit Rock Island Line*?*

Lonnie Donegan

Skiffle was a type of music which had a brief life in the 1950s. Young players who could not afford professional instruments were supposed to be able to improvise skiffle using a guitar, tea-chest bass and a washboard and thimble. Lonnie Donegan was the skiffle star. His later career was to include singing "My old man's a dustman, he wears a dustman's hat. He wears gor'blimey trousers and he lives in a council flat".

Where were the 1956 Olympic Games held?

Melbourne

These Games were threatened by the repercussions of the year's political events (the British/French invasion of Suez and the Soviet intervention in Hungary). However they were not badly affected, save in an ill-tempered water-polo semi-final between the USSR and Hungary. The hosts, Australia, did very well, dominating the swimming events. The British success was limited, but Chris Brasher won a gold in the 3,000 metres steeplechase (after appealing against a disqualification).

Which new Biblical epic starred Charlton Heston as Moses?

The Ten Commandments

Who held their first TV tea-party this year?

The *PG Tips* chimps

These well-known chimps were the stars of the longest-running series of television adverts to be shown in Britain. The next longest are *Homepride's* bowler-hatted flour graders, who first told us that "Graded grains make finer flour" in 1965. Television advertising was very different from today's very expensive, slickly-produced package. 1950s advertisements tended to feature voice-overs or stiff actors who extolled the product's qualities at great length.

When was the toddlers' truce?

From 6 pm to 7 pm

This hour had previously been set aside by the BBC for a break in television transmissions. The intention behind this was to allow mothers to have time for putting children to bed. During 1956 the government announced that it would be relaxing the restrictions on transmission during these times. In 1957 the BBC brought in the new pop music programme, *Six Five Special* to fill the 6–7 pm gap on Saturdays. The weekday gap was filled by *Tonight*.

What type of travel did British Rail abolish on 3 June?

Third class coaches

This was not the only major decision taken by the railways this year. During the 1950s, passengers were still travelling by steam engine. However it was in 1956 that the announcement was made that British Rail would be introducing electrified services. The time involved in implementing such changes meant that the decade itself would not see any of the development. The 1960s would see the completion of the first electrified line.

What new sort of nightdress was introduced after a film of this year?

The Baby Doll nightdress

Who was Trinidad's Queen of the Keyboard?

Winifred Atwell

The *Winifred Atwell Show* featured on Radio Luxembourg every Sunday at 7.30pm. The pianist played a selection of hits in her popular style, supported by Geoff Love and his Music. Teddy Johnson and Pearl Carr were on hand to sing. The show was recorded before a live audience at various venues. The first show was at Wembley Town Hall, this year. Also advertised were 'wonderful prizes given away each week'.

Which boxer retired in April, having remained undefeated as heavyweight champion of the world?

Rocky Marciano

The 33-year-old Marciano had defeated Jersey Joe Walcott for the world title and made six defences of the championship. He had also ended Joe Louis' comeback hopes. Undefeated as a professional boxer, the hard-hitting Marciano's record was 49 fights, 49 wins. Only five of his opponents survived to hear the final bell.

Who did Prince Rainer II of Monaco marry on 19 April?

Grace Kelly

The glamorous American movie queen married the monarch of the small principality of Monaco in its Roman Catholic Cathedral. The wedding was attended by more than 1,200 guests, including dignitaries from 25 nations. Television cameras were present at the lavish event and a guard of honour was provided by naval detachments from the United States and Britain.

Grace Kelly starred in the musical *High Society* during 1956. When she became Princess Grace she announced that her film career was over. Princess Grace's first child was the equally glamorous Princess Caroline.

Who wanted to Rock Around the Clock*?*

Bill Haley and the Comets

What did ERNIE pick the first ones of on 1 June?

Premium bond prize winners

Premium bonds had been introduced in the 1956 Budget and had gone on sale on 1 November of that year. (Harold Macmillan was Chancellor at the time.) These bonds earned no interest, but monthly prizes ranged from £25 to £1,000. All in all, the scheme provided a nice money earner for the government. A Labour Party spokesman called it a squalid raffle, but the next Labour government simply increased the prizes. ERNIE stood for Electronic Random Number Indicator Equipment.

Who became the first passenger to go into space and orbit the earth?

A small, black and white, Russian dog known as Laika

Laika went into orbit 1,000 miles above the earth aboard the second Russian Sputnik. The small dog ate and drank at the sound of a bell. She was strapped in with instruments monitoring her every breath and heartbeat. Laika died after a couple of days and two million miles had passed.

Laika was not the dog's name. The Russians had not thought to give it one. When asked, a spokesman had replied with the Russian for its Samoyed type, which was picked up by the western media and used incorrectly. The first man-made space satellite (Sputnik One), was launched on 4 October 1957. With this, the Soviets had taken the first step in the space race with the USA.

Who told us that we'd "never had it so good" on 20 July?

Harold Macmillan

Macmillan had become the new Tory Prime Minister on 10 January. Anthony Eden had announced his resignation the day before, owing to failing health. There were two possible replacements for Eden — Macmillan and 'Rab' Butler. A meeting of Conservative ministers chose the 62-year-old Macmillan and Butler became Home Secretary in the new government.

Macmillan's famous comment came during a speech made in Bradford. "Let's be frank about it, most of our people have never had it so good." What is sometimes forgotten is that he went on to question whether this prosperity could last and inflation could be controlled.

Who was the Royal Navy frogman whose headless body was recovered from Chichester Harbour on 26 June?

Commander Lionel 'Buster' Crabb

What hospital ward began to appear on ITV every Tuesday and Friday from February?

Emergency Ward Ten

This hospital drama was television's first twice-weekly soap opera. It enjoyed a run of nearly 10 years on ITV. Set at Oxbridge Hospital, its original characters included Dr Alan Dawson and Nurse Carole Young.

Who sang Mary's Boy Child *at Christmas this year?*

Harry Belafonte

Belafonte was a singer/actor who produced a vogue for West Indian calypso during the late 1950s. His other hit singles included *The Banana Boat Song* (1957) and *Scarlet Ribbons* (1957). He later had a success with *Hole in the Bucket* (1961).

Also in 1957, Belafonte had a hit with *Island in the Sun* which came from the film of the same name. His other films included *The World, the Flesh and the Devil* (1959). He also became active in the American civil rights movement.

Which film musical featured the song Bali Ha'i?

South Pacific

This was another 1950s musical which came from an original Rodgers and Hammerstein stage show. As with some of the other adaptations, its strongest features are the film's songs and score, which include *Some Enchanted Evening, There is Nothing Like a Dame, Younger than Springtime* and *Happy Talk*. Mitzi Gaynor starred in the film, bringing energy to songs like *I'm Gonna Wash that Man Right Outta my Hair*.

What was the horse which Frankie Laine sang about every week on television?

Champion the Wonder Horse

What sort of influenza was affecting 160 large towns by September?

Asian Flu

This virulent strain of influenza killed 39 people in the week ending 14 September. Many more people died from attacks complicated by pneumonia or bronchitis. Children were particularly affected and many were kept away from school over this period.

What well-known cube began to be wrapped in foil in 1957?

The *Oxo* cube

The cubes had previously been wrapped in card. The cost of the cube had remained at 1d through the 1920s, 1930s and 1940s. In 1952 the price had become 7½d for six. From 1957 to 1976, *Oxo's* Katie was Mary Holland. However so many people called her Katie that she changed her name to Katie Holland.

Who decided to make a television debut this Christmas?

HM The Queen

The transmission of the Queen's Christmas message underlines the spread of television. It was realized that people were not going to turn off their sets in order to listen to the Queen on the radio. Her majesty therefore made her first appearance on the small screen in 1957.

Which company launched the Victor, Cresta and Velox this year?

Vauxhall

Whose trademark was a candelabra on his grand piano?

The pianist/entertainer Liberace (pronounced Lib-er-ah-chee)

This bejewelled and besequinned television performer was well known for his outrageous clothes and pseudo-classical piano playing. His appeal lay partly in his gushing personality (though this also made him unpopular with others). In 1959 he won £8,000 from the *Daily Mirror* after its Cassandra columnist implied he was homosexual.

Whose Red Indian companion was called Tonto?

The Lone Ranger

This cowboy character featured in an early American Western television series. He had the obligatory faithful horse, Silver.

Who played Dr Simon Sparrow in a series of comedy films in the 1950s?

Dirk Bogarde

Bogarde appeared as this likeable young character in a series of *Doctor* films during the 1950s and early 1960s. This brand of light comedy proved popular in films such as *Doctor At Sea* (1955) and *Doctor In Distress* (1963). *Doctor At Sea* featured a very young Brigitte Bardot. Bogarde's other 1950s films included *The Blue Lamp* and he went on to make a variety of movies in the 1960s.

Which Preston North End and England star was elected this year's Footballer of the Year?

Tom Finney

Who were among the passengers of the British European Airways plane which crashed at Munich on 6 February?

The Manchester United football team

The Busby Babes were on their way home from a victorious European Cup Winners Cup game in Belgrade. Seven of the team were killed, several others were seriously injured. Players who lost their lives included team captain Roger Byrne and centre-forward Tommy Taylor. England left-half Duncan Edwards died from his injuries two weeks later. Survivors included team manager Matt Busby, who was seriously injured, and the young Bobby Charlton. Several journalists and club officials were also killed in the crash.

With whom did British trawlers become involved in a Cod War?

Iceland

In 1958 the Icelandic government had replaced their four-mile fishing limit with a new 12-mile boundary. British trawlers had continued to fish in the waters just outside the old limit. This had led to a number of clashes. Icelandic gunboats chased, seized and even fired at British trawlers. The Royal Navy supplied protection to the British fishing boats. At one point a navy boarding party recaptured a trawler from the Icelandic coastguard.

The problem was to reappear in the 1970s, when Iceland declared a 50-mile limit and even sank some British trawlers operating within the new limit.

In what area of London was there an outbreak of race riots on 9 September?

Notting Hill Gate

Thousands of milk bottles and a number of petrol bombs were thrown as gangs of white youths fought opposing black gangs through the night. Several people were badly hurt and 59 were charged with carrying offensive weapons and other offences. Nine youths were later jailed, each for four years. Although these troubles were not as serious as the later outbreaks (as in 1981), their effect was still significant. The occurrence of such violence came as a greater shock in 1958.

In what arab port/city was a state of emergency declared by the British this year?

Aden

Who were the stars of The Army Game?

Alfie Bass and Bill Fraser

The Army Game was an early British television comedy series. It ran from 1957 to 1962. Bill Fraser played the part of the forceful Sergeant Snudge. Alfie Bass appeared as Private Bisley, better known as Excused Boots or simply Bootsie. Because of his oddly-shaped feet, he could not wear regulation army boots and wore plimsoles instead — hence his nickname. The series ran for more than 150 episodes.

Bass and Fraser went on to star in a spin-off series which featured the characters after their demobilization — *Bootsie and Snudge.*

Who had a hit this year with You Need Hands?

Max Bygraves

Max began his career as a variety performer in the 1940s. His recording career began after he had appeared on the 1950s radio show *Educating Archie*. His hits of the decade started with *Cow-puncher's Cantata* in 1952 and included *You Need Hands* in 1958. Bygraves' career in showbusiness went on successfully into the 1970s, and was to include his hugely popular sing-along LP's and the television series *Singalong-a-Max*. His catch-phrase became "I wanna tell you a story".

Which comedian starred in his Half Hour *on both radio and television in the 1950s?*

Tony Hancock

Hancock's Half Hour began as a BBC radio show in 1954 and also became a popular television series (from 1956). Hancock's co-stars included Sid James, Hattie Jacques and Kenneth Williams. The television series ran until 1961, when, at the height of his popularity, Hancock split with James.

Tony Hancock's life came to a tragic end when he committed suicide in 1968.

What popular song and dance troupe began a television series, which was to last for over 20 years, on 14 June?

The Black and White Minstrels

What did motorists now begin to need change for?

Parking meters

Unregulated parking had become a problem in many towns. Meters were introduced as a way of controlling the difficulty. The practice of having to pay for parking was a totally new idea at the time. London's first meters appeared in 1958. Other restrictions introduced in the same year included yellow No Waiting lines.

What unusually shaped small car caught people's eyes in this year's Motor Show?

The bubble car

This small runabout gained its name from its rounded shape. It was German made, by Isetta and Messerschmitt. There were several versions but it is best remembered as a three-wheeler. The driver sat alone in the front, with one or two passengers behind. The front of the vehicle formed the door for the driver. The tiny vehicle was able to do 52 miles to the gallon. Many people felt that bubble cars were unstable and easily overturned.

What type of cigarettes nearly doubled in popularity this year?

Filter-tipped cigarettes

The start of this year had seen an early move in the health campaign against cigarettes. The British Medical Association had published a report naming cigarettes as a major cause of lung cancer. At this time, the dangers of smoking were not widely appreciated. Some advertising (*Craven A*) even made claims for cigarettes being good for the throat. However people now began to show the first signs of an awareness of smoking's health risks. The number of cigarettes sold did not fall, but there was a significant move towards filter-tipped cigarettes (£10 million worth in 1957, £18 million in 1958).

What new type of high fidelity sound, on display at this year's Radio Show, would begin to make people's current record players obsolete during the next decade?

Stereo (an innovation at this point)

Whose new army serial number was 553310761?

Elvis Presley's

Elvis began his enormously successful recording career in the 1950s. Among his hits were *Heartbreak Hotel* (1956), *All Shook Up* (1957), *Jailhouse Rock* (1958) and *A Fool Such as I* (1959). In 1958 Elvis began a much publicized two-year stint in the US Army. On his release, Elvis's singing career was even more successful, with top ten hits all through the 1960s. These included *Are You Lonesome Tonight?* (1961), *Wooden Heart* (1961), *Return to Sender* (1962), *Crying in the Chapel* (1965) and *In the Ghetto* (1969). He also made a number of films such as *GI Blues*, *Blue Hawaii* and *Girls, Girls, Girls*. Elvis wound down his recording and filming in the 1970s and in 1977 he died, aged 42.

Who was the host of This Is Your Life?

Eamonn Andrews

Andrews is best remembered as the opener of the red book on *This Is Your Life*. He appeared in this programme from its launch in 1955 until 1987, when Michael Aspel took over. He was also well known as the chairman of *What's My Line?* The genial Irishman appeared in several other broadcasting roles. These included being the first presenter of ITV's *World of Sport* and appearing on the BBC's children's programme, *Crackerjack*.

Who was the 17-year-old forward appearing for Brazil's World Cup-winning team in Stockholm?

Pele

Brazil won the 1958 World Cup when they overwhelmed host nation Sweden 5–2 in the final. The South American team, with their flying winger Garrincha and the young Pele, proved too much for the world's other sides. All four home countries had qualified for the Stockholm finals, but none managed to finish in the top four.

Who was the pint-sized Lancashire comedian who had a long-running radio show (and subsequent television series) based on his naughty boy character?

Jimmy Clitheroe

What new type of road was opened in Britain this year?

The country's first motorway, the M1

The old road system could no longer cope with heavy lorries in ever larger numbers and the continually growing road traffic of all sorts. The M1 and subsequent motorways were to make this problem easier but also ate up large amounts of farmland. The M1 is now suffering from the same problems it was built to solve: the new London–Birmingham M40 has been built because the M1 itself cannot cope with an increased volume of traffic.

Which political party won its third election in a row in 1959?

The Conservatives

Harold Macmillan led the Tories to another 1950s election victory this year. The Conservatives went to the poles before the scheduled end of their second term in office and increased their majority. This time their overall majority went up to 99 seats. The Conservatives campaigned by stressing the improved living standards during their time in office: 'Life is better with the Conservatives — Don't let Labour ruin it'.

Which racing driver was killed in a road accident on the Guildford by-pass on 22 January?

Mike Hawthorn

Twenty-nine-year-old Hawthorn had just retired after becoming world champion. The young British driver was killed driving his own sports car near his home in Surrey. Hawthorn had won at Le Mans in 1955, driving for Jaguar, though most of his Grand Prix races were to be for Ferrari. It was with Ferrari that Hawthorn clinched the world championship the previous October.

Who was the bearded revolutionary who came to power in Cuba this year?

Fidel Castro

What night did television spend at the London Palladium?

Sunday

Sunday Night at the London Palladium was a very popular variety show of the 1950s and early 1960s. It is remembered for the Beat the Clock game segment of the show and the Tiller Girls (dancers). The show had a succession of comperes, including Tommy Trinder, Bruce Forsyth, Norman Vaughan and Dickie Henderson. The show ended with the evening's guest artists waving goodbye from a revolving stage.

Who sang about a Living Doll *in 1959?*

Cliff Richard

Cliff began his long and successful singing career at the end of the 1950s. His first hit was *Move It* (1958) and his biggest 1950s record was *Living Doll*. From then on Cliff has been a consistent success on record, film and in concert. He is still a big attraction 30 years later.

   The 1960s were Cliff's biggest period of recording success, when he had 33 top ten hits, including *The Young Ones* (1962), *Bachelor Boy* (1962), *Summer Holiday* (1963) and the Eurovision Song Contest winner, *Congratulations* (1968). Cliff's films included *The Young Ones* and *Summer Holiday*. For much of this time he was backed by the Shadows, who also had some success in their own right, as with *Apache* (1960) and *Foot Tapper* (1963). Cliff's real name is Harry Webb.

What type of television programmes were Wagon Train, Gunsmoke *and* Maverick?

Western series

During the late 1950s and early 1960s Western television series were very popular. *Wagon Train* featured the adventures of families on a trek from Missouri to California, going to settle in the west. *Gunsmoke*'s chief character was Matt Dillon, Marshall of Dodge City, with his deputy, Chester. *Maverick* starred James Garner as a western gambler (who was also an ace with a gun).

Who starred as the shop steward in the Film I'm All Right Jack?

Peter Sellers

Which small car was launched on 26 August in an Austin as well as Morris version?

The Mini

Designed by Alec Issigonis, the Mini was essentially practical, with minimal styling. The controls were basic, the front windows sliding rather than winding and pull strings were used to open the doors. It was compact, inexpensive, cheap to run and capable of 70 mph. Its 1959 cost was £350 plus purchase tax in Britain of £146 9s 2d (an on-the-road price of £500). The most popular colours for the Mini in the early years were light blue and dark green. The Mini brought car ownership within reach of many who had given up hope of owning their own vehicle. Other firms responded with similar models, such as the Riley Elf and the Hillman Imp. However the Mini always proved the most popular of these small cars. By 1965, one million Minis had been produced.

What could overseas travellers now buy at Renfrew and Prestwick airports?

Duty-free wines and spirits

Passengers leaving these airports for overseas could now buy duty-free wine and spirits. Travellers were able to buy a bottle of whisky in the departure lounge. This was marked 'Not for consumption on voyage' and handed to passengers as they boarded the aircraft. Customs and Excise were initially worried that such a service would lead to an illicit home trade. However London Airport was soon to follow this example. It had been common practice abroad for several years, serving as a valuable foreign currency-earner.

What new type of washing machine became one of the latest in household aids at this time?

The twin-tub

The eventual impact made by the twin-tub can be likened to the amount of change brought about by the modern automatic machine. Washday had meant heavy work, which the spread of powered washing machines had lightened, but it still entailed a significant amount of lifting, mangling and so on. The twin-tub made the next step in work-saving, with its compact design including a spin-drier. Very few people had one at the end of the 1950s, but this was the washing machine design which manufacturers were to promote.

The next significant change in design would be the automatic machine, familiar to users in the 1990s, a logical next step in work-saving. All we need now is someone to do the ironing.

What type of swimsuit was worn by the more daring in the 1950s, but was more likely to be seen in magazines?

The bikini

Who was the captain of England's football team who played his hundredth game in April?

Billy Wright

Wright played for Wolverhampton Wanderers and was one of the stars of the 1950s. His hundredth game for England came against Scotland at Wembley, England winning 1–0. By 1959 Wright was seen as an old-fashioned player. His type of footballer was giving way to a wave of new young stars. The winning goal against Scotland had been scored by Manchester United's young forward, Bobby Charlton. In 1957 a new Chelsea player had attracted a lot of attention — the 17-year-old Jimmy Greaves. These young stars were to earn more money from the game and become better known through television coverage.

Which television personality was chosen as the Liberal candidate for Hereford in this year's General Election?

Robin Day

Day was defeated in the October Election. This was to be another very poor showing by the Liberals in a 1950s election. In 1951 they had won just six seats, fielding candidates in only one in six constituencies. In 1955 the party again held only six seats and in 1959 the Liberal vote was only 6 per cent of the total. Robin Day stayed in television.

Who chaired the new television programme Juke Box Jury?

David Jacobs

Juke Box Jury first appeared on 1 June 1959. The programme used a panel of singers, disc jockeys and ordinary viewers to judge whether new records were a Hit or a Miss. The first panel was billed as 'Alma Cogan (the popular songstress), Pete Murray (Britain's number one D-J), Gary Miller (popular recording star) and Susan Stranks (a typical teenager)'. The series was to run until 1967.

Who sang about Lipstick on Your Collar *this year?*

Connie Francis

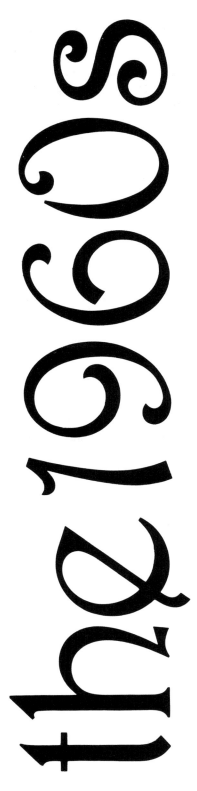

the 1960s

M ANY DEVELOPMENTS already under way in the 1950s revealed the full extent of their influence in the 1960s. This was the first complete decade to cope with the mass ownership of television and the motor car.

The number of television sets continued to grow during the 1960s, although it had already passed the 10 million mark by 1960. It had become the main form of entertainment and the primary source of news and information. Its influence went beyond changing the way people laid out their front rooms. Television altered the way people saw things. Its effect can be seen in the development of advertising. In newspapers and magazines, before mass television ownership, an advertisement would feature large areas of text which extolled the product at great length. In television advertising the cost created the need to make maximum visual impact in the minimum time. As a result, pictures grew larger and text briefer in all advertising. Advertisements in the 1960s were still a long way from today's, which make their point in one word or even without any text.

Television also had a simple effect in moulding people's memories. Before mass television ownership, people had obtained an impression of what was happening around the world through a combination of radio, cinema newsreels and newspapers. Television changed this, especially through the continued development of outside broadcasting in the 1960s. No previous decade could be recalled in the same way. Television brought a constant flow of striking images into people's front rooms. Aberfan, the *Torrey Canyon*, Vietnam and the moon landing could all be recalled in vivid images by millions of people.

The impact of mass car ownership was also fully revealed in the 1960s. Obvious environmental sacrifices were made. Motorways, urban ring roads, multistorey car parks and the private car's other effects on town planning reached new dimensions as more people were able to afford their own car. The growth in the number of cars on the roads also brought other effects, such as the change in the nature of the police force, as it moved into 'Panda' cars.

The teenage revolution which had begun in the late 1950s also developed on a larger scale in the 1960s. The teenager was the result of an economic change — during the 1930s and 1940s there had been no such creature. The difference between the periods was that the increased prosperity of the late 1950s and 1960s had led to young people having more money than ever before. Teenagers had become a market, a market substantially reflected in an explosion in the sales of records, clothes and other teenage consumer goods. The middle-aged parents of the teenagers who created Beatlemania are now amongst the elderly people of the 1990s. They will have experienced the pop boom through the behaviour of their children. 'What on earth are you wearing'?, 'Turn that noise down' and 'Get your hair cut' became popular parental phrases.

The 1960s also saw Britain's first *full* decade as a multiracial society. This often meant a difficult adjustment for both immigrant and host populations as they struggled to adapt to the realities of a newly integrated community. The continuing improvement in living standards saw the acquisition of consumer durables in ever increasing numbers. Foreign holidays (at a relatively low cost) were taken by more people and from a wider section of the community. The new Spanish resorts, such as the Costa Brava, became very popular.

Rising crime and increasing violence also became a feature of the 1960s, along with a relaxation in morals, including attitudes to divorce. The decade produced a range of characteristics which were the products of the new level of prosperity and which were recognisably more 'modern' when compared to the more conservative society of much of the 1950s. This is shown in a number of areas: the improved styling of cars and household goods; the emergence of the modern pop group and mass fashion; a newer style of political image building and electioneering (the traditional brand of Conservatism which had held power through most of 1950s Britain went into opposition for most of the 1960s). The decade was to see the emergence of colour television and other developments in media presentation, such as tabloid newspapers. The movement could even be seen in the change from the 1950s style of football kit, with its long shorts and open collars, to the round necks and modern shorts of players like Dennis Law.

Which famous novel was cleared for general sale by a jury at the Old Bailey in 1960?

Lady Chatterley's Lover

This novel by DH Lawrence had been banned in Britain for 30 years, as it had been considered obscene on account of its explicit love scenes and strong language. The book told the story of the frustrated Lady Chatterley, whose husband could not meet her sexual needs, and her gamekeeper, Mellors, who could. The publicity generated by the six-day trial did a lot to increase sales of the book. When the 3/6d Penguin paperback appeared in the bookshops, 200,000 copies were sold in one day.

The fuss made over *Lady Chatterley's Lover* now seems extraordinary, as we are surrounded by far more explicit material. However this provides a reminder of how different such standards were at the start of the 1960s.

What was Blue Streak?

A missile

Blue Streak hit the news in April 1960, when the British government announced that it would be scrapping the Blue Streak project. £65 million had been spent on developing the rocket when this decision was made. Work on Blue Streak had begun in the 1950s, when it was seen as the central weapon in Britain's independent nuclear strike force. Unfortunately by 1960 the missile's design had become obsolete. It could only be launched from a static site (Woomera in Australia had been developed) and this was at a time when it was possible to launch long-range missiles from mobile platforms. The job of making this, somewhat embarrassing, announcement fell to Harold Watkinson, the Conservative Minister of Defence.

Where were the Olympic Games held this year?

Rome

The Rome Olympics were held in the sweltering heat of a Mediterranean summer. They were the first games to receive world-wide television coverage. The British team did not do particularly well, although 19-year-old Huddersfield clerk, Anita Lonsborough, won the 200 metres breaststroke. These Games also saw the first track and field gold medal go to an African country. The unknown Ethiopian runner, Abebe Bikila, won the marathon, running barefoot.

Which cleric (once deported by the British authorities) became the first President of the Republic of Cyprus in August?

Archbishop Makarios

Who were Bernardo, Chris, Britt, Harry, Vin, Chico and Lee?

The Magnificent Seven

The number of people going to the cinema had fallen massively since the great days of the 1930s and 1940s. Cinema audiences began the decade at 9.6 million per week, having stood at 21.2 million in 1955. Many cinemas found themselves closed down or converted into bingo halls. Fewer films were made for the big screen as television came to dominate people's leisure time.

However, many good films were made in the 1960s — and of a wide variety. Westerns were still popular, 1960 producing *The Alamo*, starring John Wayne as Davy Crockett. *The Magnificent Seven* is also a Western classic. A starry cast included Charles Bronson, Yul Brynner, Steve McQueen and Robert Vaughn as four of the bad men who save a village.

Which western television series was set on the Ponderosa?

Bonanza

Bonanza was one of the most popular television westerns of the 1960s. The series concerned the life of the Cartwright family on their Ponderosa ranch. This fictional family was made up of widower Ben Cartwright and his three sons, Adam, Hoss and Little Joe. The first episode was shown in 1960 and filming went on until 1973.

What famous northern street made its first appearance in December?

Coronation Street

Set in the back streets of Salford, the first programme of this new twice-weekly soap opera went out on Friday 9 December. At first the new Wednesday and Friday serial went out on Granada television only. It was to go nationwide in May 1961. The opening scene of the first episode saw Florrie Lindley standing outside the corner shop she had just bought. It was Florrie (played by Betty Alberg), who spoke the first words of the new series. Other original characters included Ena Sharples, Minnie Caldwell, Annie Walker and Albert Tatlock. The famous street was originally to have been called Florizel Street, but a Granada TV tea lady had said it sounded more like a disinfectant. This prompted the producers to change its name to the most famous street on British television.

Who played Eric Sykes's sister in a long-running comedy partnership which began this year?

Hattie Jacques

Who received their final call-up cards in December?

National Servicemen

The compulsory calling-up of men on their eighteenth birthday to do National Service ended in 1960, after 21 years. Conscription had begun in 1939 and carried on into peacetime. Young men were selected for a compulsory two-year period of service in the armed forces. Since the war, 2.3 million men had gone through the scheme. Some men in reserved occupations (those whose jobs were important to the economy, such as miners) were exempt. Most National Servicemen went into the army — of the final batch of conscripts, 1,999 joined the army and 50 went into the RAF. After a short period of basic training, conscripts went on to units to learn a trade. The ending of National Service meant that the armed forces had to rely entirely on voluntary recruitment.

The last National Serviceman was Private RJ O'Hara.

What sort of bowling became popular in the early 1960s?

Tenpin bowling

Introduced from the United States, tenpin bowling had been known of in the 1950s, but it was only after the introduction of automatic pin spotters to Britain in 1960 that it became one of the country's fastest-growing participant sports. Many declining cinemas were now turned into bowling alleys, which became meeting places as well as simply places to go and play the new sport. Leagues were established for tenpin bowling and the sport boomed. However by the end of the decade its popularity began to wane and many bowling alleys were converted into bingo halls.

Who went on patrol for the first time in Westminster on 19 September?

Traffic wardens

Britain's first shift of traffic wardens was 39-strong and came on duty at 8am. They issued a total of 344 tickets on their first day. Wardens were introduced as a result of the Road Traffic Act 1960. By 1961 wardens had spread throughout London and into Blackpool and Leicester.

The first person to receive one of the wardens' fixed-penalty tickets was Dr Thomas Creighton. He had parked his Ford Popular outside a hotel while he treated a patient suffering from a heart attack. The first person to issue a ticket had been Warden Frank Shaw, who did not know that the car belonged to a doctor. Because of the publicity given to this incident, Dr Creighton did not have to pay his £2 fixed penalty.

How did the National Health Service begin to help your hearing from 7 June?

By issuing the first NHS hearing-aids

Who was shot down by the Russians on 1 May?

Gary Powers

Powers was the pilot of an American U2 spy plane which was shot down by Soviet fighters over Sverdlovsk. He was found guilty of spying and sentenced to 10 years' imprisonment. However Powers was released in 1962, when he was exchanged for a Soviet spy. After his return to the United States, Powers became a civilian helicopter pilot. He was killed in 1977 when his helicopter crashed.

Which motor racing driver lost his licence in April for dangerous driving?

Stirling Moss

Moss had won his first Grand Prix in 1955, beating world champion Juan Fangio to take the British Grand Prix. Through the second half of the 1950s he clocked up other Grand Prix wins at Monaco, Portugal and Italy. In 1958 he was runner-up to Mike Hawthorn in the world championship.

The 1960s brought more driving success, but this was accompanied by an embarrassing driving ban (for one year) in 1960. This was followed by a 110 mph crash, before a Bank Holiday crowd at Goodwood in 1962, which left Moss with a broken leg and serious head injuries.

Who married Mr Anthony Armstrong-Jones in Westminster Abbey on Friday 6 May?

Princess Margaret

This was the biggest royal wedding of the 1960s. Two thousand guests were inside the Abbey and the streets outside were lined with people hoping to catch a glimpse of the Princess. Millions more watched the event on television and school children were given a day off school to mark the event. Princess Margaret became the first 'Royal' for 450 years to marry a commoner. The Duke of Edinburgh gave away the 29-year-old Princess, who wore a Norman Hartnell-designed dress made of white silk organza. She had eight bridesmaids, including Princess Anne. The marriage was dissolved in 1978.

Who was the woman doctor who did much to popularize the new craze for long-distance walking?

Dr Barbara Moore

How much did the Fulham footballer, Johnny Haynes, begin to earn in 1961?

£100 per week

The Fulham captain was to become Britain's first £100 per week player in 1961. This was to be a decade of spiralling wages for soccer stars: gone were the days of the maximum wage. Transfer fees also reached unheard of levels. Denis Law became Britain's most expensive player in 1960, after he had moved from Huddersfield Town to Manchester City for £55,000. Law became Britain's first £100,000 player when he moved to Turino of Italy in 1961.

What did Great Britain apply to join in August (but unsuccessfully)?

The Common Market (European Economic Community)

The Common Market had been formed in 1957, when Italy, France, West Germany, Belgium, Netherlands and Luxembourg signed the Treaty of Rome. Britain was not a founder member and there were to be years of debate before she did join. The UK's first application to join was in 1961. This attempt was eventually blocked by the French president, General De Gaulle. In 1967, De Gaulle again said 'Non' to British membership.

It was only in 1973 that Britain became a full member of the EEC. This was after Ted Heath had negotiated membership. Even after this, Britain was to hold a referendum on its membership (in 1975) following the Labour Party's defeat of Heath's Conservative government. Two-thirds of the British people voted to stay in the EEC.

What began to be built in Germany on the morning of 13 August?

The Berlin Wall

The border between East and West Berlin had been closed in 1960. It was not until the following year that East German soldiers divided the sectors with barbed wire. Some 50,000 East Germans who worked in the West were not allowed to pass. Work was soon to start on the building of the 28¼-mile wall, which was to divide the city for nearly 30 years. The wall was made with prefabricated concrete blocks and was heavily guarded by the East Germans. Over the years, many people tried to escape from the Communist East to the West and many were shot trying to make their way across the wall.

What was the expensive (at £2,196 19s 2d), high-performance sports car introduced by Jaguar in March?

The E-type Jaguar

Which new television series featured John Steed?

The Avengers

This fantasy crime/adventure series made its debut in 1961. Steed (played by Patrick MacNee) was assisted by a series of glamorous female helpers. The first of these was Kathy Gale (Honor Blackman) who was well known for her leather outfits and judo skills. The second was Emma Peel (Diana Rigg). Steed himself was famous for his pin-striped suits and steel-rimmed bowler.

Which musical included the songs Tonight, I Feel Pretty *and* Somewhere?

West Side Story

Originally a stage musical, *West Side Story* won the Oscar for best film in 1961. Music was by Leonard Bernstein and lyrics by Stephen Sondheim. Many of the cast were new to the movies. An often forgotten contribution was made by Marni Nixon, who dubbed Natalie Wood's voice. Marni Nixon also dubbed for Audrey Hepburn in *My Fair Lady* and Deborah Kerr in *The King and I*. The film's story is an updated version of *Romeo and Juliet* featuring the rivalry of two gangs, the Sharks and the Jets.

Which television Western series featured a character called Rowdy Yates?

Rawhide

This popular television western featured the adventures of a cattle drive. Rowdy Yates was played by a young Clint Eastwood (later to become a movie superstar). The series had a well-known theme tune, sung by Frankie Laine ('Rolling, rolling, rolling, keep them dogies rolling . . .').

Which bowler-hatted clarinet player had a huge hit this year with Stranger On The Shore?

Acker Bilk

What sort of shop was made legal on 1 May?

The betting shop

In 1960, betting shops were not supposed to exist. The only legal betting was on-course betting. Off-track gambling on race horses did take place, but such activities were carried on underground. Such off-course betting was legalized by the Betting and Gaming Act and this made betting shops legal. The first of these opened in London, though they were not easy to find because they were not allowed to display prominent advertising.

What dance caught on in Britain after the release of a Chubby Checker record?

The twist

This was the biggest dance craze of the 1960s and is still popular today. The record *Let's Twist Again* was released in 1961 and spent 34 weeks in the charts. Although there were other short dance crazes, such as the mashed potato, the twist is *the* dance of the 1960s.

What bird was shown on the reverse of a farthing?

A wren

The farthing was one of the smallest British coins ever minted, worth one quarter of an old penny (960 farthings to the pound). On 1 January 1961 the farthing ceased to be legal tender. It was a cause of annoyance to many people because it was so easy to lose.

Which mother and baby suppliers opened their very first shop on 14 September in Kingston, Surrey?

Mothercare

Which popular woman singer was brought up in the Tiger Bay area of Cardiff?	**Shirley Bassey** The two songs with which Shirley Bassey is most often associated are *Big Spender* and *Goldfinger* (the theme from a James Bond film). She also enjoyed much recording success between 1957 and 1973. This included the 1960s hits *What Now My Love?* and *I (Who Have Nothing)*. In 1961 she had a number one hit with *Reach for the Stars*.
Who became the first man in space during this year?	**Major Yuri Gagarin** The Russians surprised most people when they were first to put a man into space. Gagarin's pioneering flight lasted for only 108 minutes. Having come through the flight unharmed, he became a Hero of the Soviet Union. He was well received by all the countries he visited after making his historic flight. Ironically, Gagarin was to die in an air-crash during a routine training flight.
Who became the first person to refuse to appear on This is Your Life?	**Danny Blanchflower** (footballer) Blanchflower was the captain of Tottenham Hotspur's 1960/61 FA Cup and League title-winning side. Spurs were the first twentieth-century side to do the double. Blanchflower also played many games for Northern Ireland. He refused to appear on the popular television programme in February of 1961.
Which glamorous Italian movie star, married to director Carlo Ponti, starred in El Cid?	**Sophia Loren**

Who became the manager of the England football team this year?

Alf Ramsey

Alf Ramsey was the manager of the England international team when they won the World Cup in 1966. He was first appointed to the job in 1962 in place of Walter Winterbottom. As a player, Ramsey had been a full-back for Southampton and 'Spurs' in the early 1950s. He also appeared 32 times for England. After retiring as a player, Ramsey became manager of Third Division team Ipswich Town. He took them to the First Division and the League title by 1962. This success made him the obvious choice as the new England boss.

What new form of transport began its first regular passenger service on the Dee estuary in July?

The hovercraft

This first service operated between Wallasey and Rhyl, starting on 20 July. The first regular cross-Channel service (Ramsgate–Calais) began in 1966. In 1968 the Channel hoverferry service began. The *Princess Margaret*, which made the first crossing, was capable of carrying 30 cars and 254 passengers. The hovercraft's designer, Christopher Cockerell, was knighted in 1969.

What did a number of people try to beat by flying into Britain before the end of July?

The 1962 Immigration Act

In the two years from 1959 to 1961 the number of immigrants into Britain from Commonwealth countries increased five-fold, from 21,000 to 100,000. The government now announced a new Immigration Bill. This prevented absolute freedom of entry for Commonwealth immigrants, who now needed a voucher showing that they had a job to come to or possessed useful skills. This Act was followed by the 1968 Act, which imposed strict penalties for helping illegal immigrants, and the 1971 Bill which more or less ended the inalienable rights of Commonwealth workers to settle in Britain.

What island off America was in the news when it was found to be allowing nuclear missile bases to be built?

Cuba

Who played James Bond in the first of the Bond films?

Sean Connery

The fantasy espionage character of James Bond had been created in the books of Ian Fleming. He was brought to the big screen in the 1960s, with Connery first playing Agent 007 in *Doctor No* (1962). Sean Connery went on to appear as Bond in *From Russia With Love* (1963), *Goldfinger* (1964), *Thunderball* (1965) and *You Only Live Twice* (1967). George Lazenby played Bond once, in *On Her Majesty's Secret Service* (1969), but Roger Moore took over the role in the 1970s and 1980s.

Who was the well-known television doctor played by Richard Chamberlain?

Dr Kildare

Two hundred episodes of the American hospital series, *Dr Kildare*, were shown between 1961 and 1966. Kildare was played by a new young actor, Richard Chamberlain, who became a 1960s heart-throb. The series had a large audience, many of whom were women. Even 20 years later, Chamberlain could attract a sizeable female following for his part in *The Thorn Birds*. *Dr Kildare* also featured Raymond Massey as Dr Gillespie. The series' theme-tune reached the British charts in 1962.

Who had the catch-phrase, 'Just like that'?

Tommy Cooper

Cooper was a popular magician/comedian. His act was best known for the way in which he messed up his attempts at magic tricks, although, in reality, Cooper was a talented magician. Tommy was also famous for his red fez and the faces he pulled during his disastrous tricks. He was a regular television and stage performer during the 1960s and 1970s. Tommy Cooper died in 1984, aged 62, after collapsing on stage during a live television programme.

Which down-to-earth Scotsman became manager of the recently promoted Liverpool soccer team this year?

Bill Shankley

What sort of fashion was a 'beehive'?

A hairstyle

The beehive was a popular women's hairstyle of the 1960s. Hair was back-combed (teased) into the required height, then held in place by a generous use of lacquer. The eventual effect resembled a beehive shape, hence the name. By putting their hair into a 'beehive' and wearing stiletto-heel shoes, fairly small women could add several inches to their height, achieving a somewhat misleading effect.

What covered London for five days from 3 December?

Smog

December 1962 saw Britain covered in the worst fog for 10 years. In London this took the form of smog. The amount of smoke and sulphur dioxide in the London air was much greater than normal, which led to 800 people being admitted to hospital with chest and heart conditions; 60 actually died. Smog masks were worn by many as people coped with very poor visibility in the metropolitan area. Traffic was minimal, while the Port of London and Heathrow Airport came to a standstill. Action taken to promote cleaner air has greatly reduced the dangers of smog.

What made its first five-minute appearance in June?

Police Five

Britain's first aid-the-police series was devised in order to fill a five-minute programme gap. It began on 30 June in the London area. Shaw Taylor presented the first programme, in liaison with Scotland Yard. The programme was assisted by the new identikit technique (introduced in 1961) which became a vital part of police detection work. The first suspected criminal to be caught through the new invention was Edwin Bush.

What was different about the filling station opened on London's Southwark Bridge this year?

It was Britain's first self-service station

Who was the blind singer who topped the charts with I Can't Stop Loving You?

Ray Charles

Blind from the age of six, Ray Charles went on to be a successful singer/musician in several styles: rhythm and blues, soul, jazz and pop. He also sang Country and Western, something rare for a black musician. Charles was always more successful in the United States, though he did have other British hits with *Hit The Road, Jack* (1961) and *Take These Chains From My Heart* (1963). Though his recording success was limited to the early 1960s, before the new groups took over, he went on to be a popular cabaret performer.

Who was the singer with a yodelling voice who had a big hit this year with I Remember You?

Frank Ifield

This was one of Frank's four number one hits in the early 1960s. The others were *Lovesick Blues* (1962), *Wayward Wind* (1963) and *Confessin'* (1963). Ifield's records were very successful over a short period. Like many other singers, he had little recording success after the groups took over, but went on to have a long career in cabaret. Many people think that Frank Ifield is Australian. He had emigrated to Australia and appeared on Australian radio and television, but he originally came from Coventry, having been born there in 1937.

Who played Lawrence of Arabia in the epic movie of the same name?

Peter O'Toole

Lawrence of Arabia was three and three-quarter hours long and told the story of TE Lawrence. It was awarded the 1962 Oscar for best film. Other stars included Anthony Quinn, Jack Hawkins and Omar Shariff. Peter O'Toole appeared in many movies during the 1960s. These included *Becket* (1964), *What's New Pussycat?* (1965), *The Night of the Generals* (1967) and *The Lion in Winter* (1968).

Who was hanged, perhaps wrongly, for the 'A6 murders'?

James Hanratty

What happened at 3.10 am on 8 August, on the Glasgow–London railway line?

The 'Great Train Robbery'

This has become the most famous robbery in British history. It was carried out on the Glasgow to London mail train which was carrying over two and a half million pounds in used bank notes (on their way to London to be destroyed). A large, well organized gang carried out the raid in Buckinghamshire. Five days after the robbery, following a huge police operation, the gang were captured at their Leatherslade Farm hideout. Their trial began at Buckinghamshire Assizes on 20 January. Twelve of the gang were eventually given a total of 307 years' imprisonment.

Two of the robbers escaped from prison: Charlie Wilson was recaptured in Canada in 1968, but Ronnie Biggs is still free and is living in Brazil. Buster Edwards has had a film made about his exploits. Train driver Jack Mills died a few years after the raid as a result of head injuries sustained during the robbery.

Who replaced Harold Macmillan as Leader of the Conservative Party?

Sir Alec Douglas-Home

Douglas-Home was a surprise choice as Macmillan's replacement. When he took over as Tory leader he was not even an MP. A month after his appointment he was elected to the Commons after winning the Kinross by-election. He also renounced his peerage and became plain Alec Douglas-Home. Douglas-Home was to last only a short time as Prime Minister, as the Conservatives lost the 1964 election.

Who was Lee Harvey Oswald supposed to have shot on 22 November?

President Kennedy

John Fitzgerald Kennedy, thirty-fifth President of the United States, was assassinated in Dallas, Texas. He was on his way to make a speech, travelling in an open-topped car with his wife Jackie and the Governor of Texas. The car was hit by a hail of bullets and 25 minutes later Kennedy was dead from head wounds. This was one of the most sensational news stories of the whole decade.

Lee Harvey Oswald was arrested that day, charged with a different shooting. Although he denied all knowledge of the President's assassination, he was also charged with Kennedy's killing. Before he could go for trial he was shot and killed by Dallas night-club owner, Jack Ruby, who was convinced of his guilt. There is now considerable doubt as to who was the President's killer.

What revolutionary aid to family planning became available on prescription in June 1963?

The contraceptive pill

As whom was Simon Templar also known?

The Saint

The new television series *The Saint* made its debut in 1963, following the adventures of private detective Simon Templar. The world of the *The Saint*, much like that of James Bond, was filled with attractive girls and fast cars. Significantly, Simon Templar was played by Roger Moore, who went on to play Bond as well. The 114th and final episode of the original series was filmed in 1968.

Maurice Micklewhite was one of the stars of this year's film success, Zulu. *As whom is he better known?*

Michael Caine

Caine had previously had a number of minor film roles, but his big break came when he played one of the officers in *Zulu*. He went on to appear regularly in 1960s films. These included *The Ipcress File* (1965), in which he played spy Harry Palmer, *Alfie* (1966), where he played the philandering hero, and *The Italian Job* (1969), where he played crook Charlie Croker. Caine's success continued through the 1970s and 1980s. In 1984 he was nominated for an Oscar following his performance as a drunken lecturer in *Educating Rita*.

Caine's real name was changed in the 1950s. It certainly lacks the ring needed for star billing.

Who were John, Paul, George and Ringo?

The Beatles

John Lennon, Paul McCartney, George Harrison and Ringo Starr made up the best-known pop group of the 1960s and had an enormous influence on the decade's fashion and entertainment. The group's first success came in the early 1960s. In 1963 they had three number one records: *From Me To You, I Want To Hold Your Hand* and *She Loves You*. They were to have 14 more number ones over the decade.

In the early 1960s, the group was followed everywhere by hysterical young fans. These screaming youngsters are now in their forties as we enter the 1990s. Beatlemania produced all sorts of fashion spin-offs — Beatle haircuts, Beatle jackets and Beatle boots. The Liverpool group also appeared in films (such as *A Hard Day's Night*) in the mid-1960s. The music was great, the films were dreadful. As the decade progressed, the Beatles changed with it, producing music all through the sixties which was hugely popular with younger people.

Which Alfred Hitchcock film of this year featured people being attacked by thousands of non-human extras?

The Birds

How much was the Average Weekly Wage in 1963?*

£16 14s 11d

*This is based on the earnings of manual workers over the age of 21. Wages and prices during the 1960s were relatively stable (though not seen as such at the time). The average wage rose from £14 10s 8d (1960) to £24 16s 5d (1969). The inflation rate varied between 2 per cent (1963) and 5.4 per cent (1969). This stability, like that of the 1950s, was a far cry from the runaway price and wage rises of the later 1970s. (In August 1979, inflation was to reach 26.9 per cent.)

What did Horace Batchelor have a system for winning?

The football pools

Horace invited you to win with his famous system in advertisements on Radio Luxembourg. He called his system *In For a Draw* and punters wrote to him at PO Box number six, Keynsham, Bristol. Batchelor did have some success (over a thousand first dividends for himself and many more for his system's users). The question remains as to how many people had to lose with the system for this success to be achieved.

Of what did Dr Beeching recommend closing 2,000?

Railway stations

Beeching was Chairman of British Railways between 1961 and 1965. He is best remembered for the famous Beeching Report of 1963. This suggested a concentration of rail services on inter-city passenger routes. What Beeching was doing was catching up on a society which no longer depended so heavily on its railway network for transport. The motor car and road freight especially threatened the need for many branch lines, now far less used.

Beeching's report was called *The reshaping of British Railways*. It recommended the closure of 2,000 stations and a reduction of 5,000 miles of the rail network. Many branch lines were closed. Disused lines, closed as a result of Beeching's report, can be seen in many parts of the country. The closures outlined by Beeching were carried out from 1964 onwards.

What rear-engined car was launched by Rootes this year?

The Hillman Imp

Who floored Cassius Clay at the end of the fourth round in their fight at Wembley?

Henry Cooper

Our 'Enery was one of Britain's most popular sporting figures in the 1960s. He had first become British heavyweight boxing champion in 1959 and European champion in 1964. Clay (not yet world champion) had arrived in London in his usual confident mood, saying he would finish Cooper off in five rounds. He was to get a shock when Cooper knocked him down at the end of the fourth. Clay was visibly shaken, but between rounds he claimed to have a torn glove; this gave him a much-needed breathing space and he came out fresh for the next round, when he defeated Cooper. The two men met again in 1966, this time for the world title. Cooper was defeated again, retiring in the sixth round with bad cuts.

Which Government Minister was forced to resign by scandal in June?

John Profumo

Profumo was Secretary of State for War. The scandal which led to his resignation filled the newspapers at the time. It was alleged that the Minister had been having a relationship with Christine Keeler who, at the same time, was involved with the Russian Naval attaché Eugene Ivanov. Profumo at first denied this, but ten weeks later he admitted the truth. Profumo went on to reveal an involvement with a circle of people, including Keeler, Mandy Rice-Davies and Stephen Ward (who was later charged with living off immoral earnings).

Which busty blonde burst her bra in Carry On Camping?

Barbara Windsor

The first *Carry On* film had appeared in 1958 and the popular comedies continued to be made until the early 1970s. During the 1960s, their brand of saucy slapstick proved a great box-office success. The regular stars of *Carry On* films included Kenneth Williams, Charles Hawtrey, Sid James, Barbara Windsor and Joan Sims. Among the many titles were *Carry on Nurse*, *Carry on Cleo*, *Carry on up the Khyber* and *Carry on Cowboy*.

Who did Viscount Stansgate become when he took advantage of the new Peerage Bill to renounce his title?

Anthony Wedgewood-Benn

What replaced the Daily Herald *on 14 September?*

The *Sun*

The *Sun* was Britain's first new national daily newspaper for 34 years. Its first edition had 24 pages and the front page showed Alec Douglas-Home during his election campaign. The *Daily Herald* published its last edition on the same day. The *Herald*'s future had looked bleak in the previous year when very substantial losses were announced. On its first day the *Sun* sold three and a half million copies. By its last day the *Herald* sold an average of 1.3 million per day. The original *Sun* was not a tabloid paper and was very different from the *Sun* of today which we all know and love. It became a tabloid paper at the end of the decade (November 1969).

Who occupied the new Centre Point office block in London during 1964?

No one

Centre Point was one of the scandals of the 1960s. It attracted a great deal of attention because it remained unoccupied for the whole decade, at a time when there was great concern over the number of homeless people in the capital. Built in 1964, the 34-storey building was not to be occupied until 1979, when the CBI (Confederation of British Industries) made its headquarters there.

Who became Prime Minister in 1964 and was famous for pipe-smoking and wearing a Gannex raincoat?

Harold Wilson

Wilson had taken over as leader of the Labour Party in 1963, following the death of Hugh Gaitskell. He became Prime Minister after the 1964 election, ending 13 consecutive years of Conservative government. Labour's majority was only four seats. The party's total vote had actually fallen since 1959, but a significant swing to the Liberals took votes away from the Conservatives.

Wilson was the MP for the Huyton constituency. A constant support to him was his wife Mary. He also relied much on his political secretary, Marcia Williams, whom he controversially made Lady Falkender upon his retirement.

In which Olympic Games did Welsh schoolteacher, Lynn Davies, win a gold medal in the long jump?

Tokyo

What musical featured the songs I Could Have Danced All Night, The Rain in Spain *and* On the Street Where You Live?

My Fair Lady

This film won the best-film Oscar for 1964. The musical was based on George Bernard Shaw's play *Pygmalion*. The story concerns a wager between Professor Higgins (Rex Harrison) and Pickering (Wilfred Hyde-White) as to whether Higgins can educate and reform the character of a typical market-girl (Eliza Doolittle). The girl is played by Audrey Hepburn.

Which fictional motel was first seen on 2 November (but only in the Midlands)?

Crossroads

Midlands television viewers were first able to see the *Crossroads* soap opera in 1964. The rest of the nation had to wait until 1972 before Meg Richardson, Amy Turtle and Benny were networked. Like *Coronation Street*, the motel was thought initially only to have a regional appeal. Another similarity with *Coronation Street* is that *Crossroads* had a different original working title — *Midland Road*.

Which Irish trio sang about Diane and Ramona this year?

The Bachelors

Three Dublin lads, the brothers Con and Dec Clusky and John Stokes made up the Bachelors. They had several hits during the 1960s but in a style very different from that of the new groups. Their first chart success was *Charmaine* (1963); other hits were *I Believe* (1964) and *I Wouldn't Trade You For The World* (1964).

What new television comedy series featured a witch called Samantha?

Bewitched

What began to broadcast on 21 April?

BBC 2

The BBC's second television channel should have been launched the previous night but a fire at Battersea Power Station had delayed its first broadcast. The new station's first programme was *Play School*. The new channel was not a great success in its early days, but in 1965 the quality of programme began to improve. Several programmes were piloted on the new channel before being transferred to BBC1, among them *The Likely Lads*, which featured Rodney Bewes and James Bolam as two young lads from the North East.

What fashion sensation was several inches above the knee in 1964?

The miniskirt

It is not quite clear who originally designed the miniskirt, but hemlines were on the way up in 1964. By 1965 skirts six inches above the knee were common. The mini brought a temporary end to the days of stockings and suspenders and a boom in the sale of tights.

What did Kenneth Wolstenholme introduce for the first time ever on 22 August?

Match of the Day

This was the start of a regular Saturday night ritual for millions of men over the country. Soon Saturday night would be incomplete without *Match of the Day*. At first, the experimental programme appeared on BBC2, but it was soon moved to BBC1. The first game to be covered was Liverpool's 3–2 defeat of Arsenal. Liverpool's Roger Hunt scored the first goal to be seen on *Match of the Day.*

Which two groups of youths, travelling on scooters and motorbikes, caused fighting, vandalism and 51 arrests in Margate on 18 May?

Mods and Rockers

Who became Elizabeth Taylor's fifth husband?

Richard Burton

Burton was an acclaimed stage actor who also made regular films over the 1960s. These varied in quality, and included *The Longest Day* (1962), *The Night of the Iguana* (1964), *The Spy Who Came in from the Cold* (1965), *Who's Afraid of Virginia Woolf?* (1966), *Where Eagles Dare* (1968) and *Anne of the Thousand Days* (1969). Throughout the rest of the decade he regularly made the news because of his romance with and marriage to Elizabeth Taylor. He had met the movie queen on the set of *Cleopatra* in 1962. The subsequent romance cost Burton a tidy sum, especially when he bought Liz the 33-carat Krupp diamond. Their much-publicized marriage lasted 10 years and was followed by a short remarriage.

Who was the popular Country and Western singer who died in a plane crash on 31 July?

Jim Reeves

Reeves sold millions of records during the 1960s, even though his style of singing was not at all fashionable. His music appealed to an older audience. Before his death he had British success with *Welcome to My World* (1963) and *I Love You Because* (1964). After the plane crash, he had posthumous hits with *There's a Heartache Following Me* and his only number one, *Distant Drums* (1966). Reeves' music remains popular today as his records continue to sell.

Who ran a rag and bone business from Oil Drum Lane, Shepherd's Bush?

Steptoe and Son

This very popular comedy series had its own regular slot from 1964. It featured Wilfred Brambell and Harry H Corbett as father and son. Much of the series' humour was based upon Harold's constant ambitions to move on to something more up-market than the rag and bone trade. His ambitions were always thwarted by his scheming old father. The pair carried out their business with the help of Hercules, who pulled their cart. The series was to continue for nearly 10 years.

Who had a big hit this year when she sang Downtown?

Petula Clark

What was opened on 8 October and was 619 feet tall?

The Post Office Tower

When Prime Minister Harold Wilson opened this 30-storey tower it was the tallest building in Britain. Situated in Bloomsbury, the tower could handle 150,000 telephone calls simultaneously and cope with 40 television channels. A rotating restaurant and viewing galleries were opened to the public in 1966.

Who escaped from London Zoo in March?

Goldie the eagle

Goldie had two spells of freedom in 1965. His first lasted for 10 days and aroused much newspaper and public interest. The seven-year-old golden eagle set up home in Regent's Park, where thousands came to see him. Attempts to recapture the bird all failed until he succumbed to the temptation of food. Goldie made a second escape in December, but this time was recaptured after four days.

What was abolished by Parliament on 8 November?

Hanging

On this date, the Murder Bill (Abolition of the Death Penalty) became law. This ended the death penalty for murder. The last people to be executed in Britain had been Peter Anthony Allen (21) and John Robson Walby (24). They had both been convicted of murder and their executions were carried out simultaneously on 13 August 1964: Allen's at Walton Prison Liverpool, Walby's at Strangeways in Manchester.

For what country did Ian Smith make a Unilateral Declaration of Independence (UDI) on 11 November?

Rhodesia (now Zimbabwe)

Which Liverpool comedian was well-known for his tickling stick?

Ken Dodd

Dodd was a comedian/singer who was known for his protruding teeth and stand-up hair. He was often accompanied on stage by his characters Dickie Mint and the Diddy Men. His catch-phrases included "Where's me shirt?" and "Have you ever been tickled, missus?" As well as his comic act, Dodd had a good singing voice. His records included the 1965 hit *Tears*, one of the best-selling records of the decade.

Who patrolled the streets of Newtown?

Z Cars

The popular police series *Z Cars* ran for more than 650 episodes and lasted for 18 years. The series was centred around the workings of Newtown police station and the Panda cars Z Victor 1 and Z Victor 2. Central figures in the episodes included Detective Inspector Barlow and Sergeant Watt.

Which film musical included the songs My Favourite Things, Climb Every Mountain *and* Edelweiss?

The Sound of Music

This musical was the biggest box-office success of the 1960s. It also won the 1965 Oscar for best film. The LP of the soundtrack sold an all-time record 14 million copies. The film was based on the story of Maria, who quits her convent life to become governess to Captain von Trapp's children. As in all good musicals, she falls in love with the hero. Julie Andrews played Maria and Christopher Plummer was Captain von Trapp.

Which Welshman with a hairy chest had a hit song this year with It's Not Unusual?

Tom Jones

Who was the housewife and clean-up-TV campaigner in the news in November?

Mrs Mary Whitehouse

Mrs Whitehouse was a self-appointed spokeswoman for the silent majority. In 1965 she set up the National Viewers' and Listeners' Association, which she claimed was formed to tackle 'bad taste and irresponsibility' in the media. How representative Mrs Whitehouse was of anyone's opinions was always in question and she became a byword for prudery. However a significant number of people were concerned about a fall in moral standards. It is interesting to compare what shocked people then with the television and movie standards of today. We are accustomed to swearing in television drama. Fairly explicit sex scenes are shown on network television films and plays. This was not the case in the early 1960s.

What could many workers now expect to receive if they lost their jobs?

Redundancy pay

Under the terms of the new Redundancy Payments Act, workers made redundant now had the right to expect extra payments from their employers. The amount depended upon salary and length of employment.

The 1950s and 1960s fostered new attitudes to work. Increased welfare benefits and, more importantly, the availability of plenty of jobs made the threat of unemployment much less of a concern to people. Better and more accessible health care also removed the fear of sickness (or rather, the implications of sickness) that had been part of many people's lives in the pre-war years.

What previously run-down back street near Regent Street became a well-known young people's fashion centre in the 1960s?

Carnaby Street

Fashionable clothes for young people began to be sold in a new type of clothes shop during the 1960s. Boutiques encouraged new fashion trends, one of which was the movement towards the fashion-conscious man as well as woman. This has continued and developed ever since (although roll-necked pullovers and Cuban-heeled boots are not in fashion any more).

Another effect of boutiques was to make fashions more transient. The miniskirt was followed by the maxi, which was followed by the midi. Clothes would now increasingly be left in the wardrobe simply because they weren't the thing to wear any more.

In the 1960s, fashions became something young people actually wore, rather than read about in magazines. Carnaby Street was a collection of boutiques which attracted a lot of media attention.

What was banned from British television screens in August?

Cigarette advertising

What did Cassius Clay change his name to?

Muhammad Ali

Known for bombarding his opponents with abuse and claiming that he was the greatest, Ali was one of the most controversial sporting figures of the 1960s. Some people did not like his extrovert behaviour, but there was no denying his talent as a boxer. He first won the world title in 1964, when he beat Sonny Liston, despite being very much the underdog. The following year, Ali met Liston again. This time he knocked out his opponent in one minute to retain his title.

In between these two fights, Clay had become a Muslim, changing his name to Muhammad Ali. Ali went on to make eight more title defences in the 1960s. In 1967 he was stripped of his title after being sentenced to a prison term (which he never served) for failing to join the US forces and serve in Vietnam. Ali came back to regain the title in 1974 and again in 1978.

Which leading Conservative sailed a yacht called Morning Cloud?

Ted Heath

In July 1965, Heath succeeded Sir Alec Douglas-Home as leader of the Tories. The Ted Heath–Harold Wilson rivalry featured strongly in popular reporting of 1960s politics. Heath became Prime Minister in 1970, after the Conservatives' General Election success. His characteristic, shoulder-jerking laugh made him a target for impersonators and comedians.

Which television science fiction hero was first played by William Hartnell?

Doctor Who

The Doctor had first been seen in 1963. He travelled through time by Tardis (which outwardly took the form of a police telephone box). A fault had developed in the Tardis and the Doctor was unable to predict the time and location of his next landing. This took the Doctor, his niece Susan and their companion Ian into various adventures. They were also confronted by a number of grotesque monsters. The most popular of these were the Daleks, who were introduced in the second series. These gelatinous masses were encased in metal buggies equipped with lasers and other weapons. They were famous for the cry "exterminate, exterminate", made with their synthesized voices.

The Doctor has since been played by Patrick Troughton, Jon Pertwee, Tom Baker, Peter Davidson and Sylvester McCoy. The programme's catchy theme tune (developed by the BBC's sound workshop) has helped to maintain a degree of continuity.

Who were the 'Moors murderers'?

Myra Hindley and Ian Brady

What happened at Aberfan on 21 October?

The village school was buried under tons of slurry which slid down from a rain-soaked coal tip

This was one of Britain's most tragic disasters and one of the 1960s' most memorable events. This Welsh village lost 116 children and 28 adults as they were buried alive under the moving coal slurry. Rescue workers formed human chains and managed to bring a few children out alive, but soon they began to bring out dead bodies. The small village lost almost a whole generation of children when the school was buried.

Whose strike led the Prime Minister to declare a state of emergency on 23 May?

The seamen's strike

The dispute between the National Union of Seamen and their employers was over the length of the working week without overtime. At the time it was 56 hours and the NUS wanted it to be 40. The state of emergency was declared to ensure the maintenance of essential supplies and services during the mounting congestion in the ports. Wilson, the Prime Minister, accused the strike's leaders of being under Communist influence. The dispute ended on 1 July.

Who found the stolen World Cup on Sunday 20 March?

Pickles

Pickles was a small mongrel dog who was out for a walk with his owner, David Corbell, in Norwood, South London. He found the 12-inch high gold trophy, wrapped in newspaper, in the garden of a house. The famous soccer trophy had been stolen from its locked cabinet when on display at the Central Hall, Westminster. Pickles managed to outdo an extensive police hunt and earned his owner a £6,000 reward.

Which political party won the 1966 General Election?

The Labour Party

Who appeared in his television shows sitting in his famous rocking chair?

Val Doonican

This clean-cut Irishman's pleasant personality and easy-going brand of light entertainment appealed to young and old alike. He sang ballads such as *Walk Tall* and occasional comedy songs such as *Paddy McGinty's Goat* and *Delaney's Donkey*. Doonican had success on the small screen and on record. This year saw chart success with *Elusive Butterfly*.

Which Liverpool lass sang the theme song from the film Alfie?

Cilla Black

Cilla had changed colour in 1963, when she gave up her old name of Priscilla White. Her first big record success came in 1964, with *Anyone Who Had a Heart* and *You're My World*. *Anyone Who Had a Heart* was the biggest-selling single for a female singer in the 1960s. She had several other hits during the decade, such as *You've Lost that Lovin' Feelin'* (1965) and *Step Inside Love* (1968). Towards the end of the decade she began to diversify into television variety. This has included her own show and, recently, *Blind Date* and *Surprise Surprise!* Cilla has certainly come a long way from the 21-year-old ex-typist who first sang to us in 1964.

Who scored a hat trick for England in the World Cup final?

Geoff Hurst

The 1966 World Cup was held in England. A fitting climax came when England met West Germany in the final at Wembley. The England team was: Banks, Cohen, Wilson, Stiles, J Charlton, Moore, Ball, Hurst, Hunt, R Charlton, Peters. England won the game 4–2, but only after West Germany had forced extra time with an equalizer in injury time.

The West Ham forward, Geoff Hurst, put England back in front with a very controversial goal. His shot hit the underside of the bar and bounced back into play. After consulting the linesman, the referee awarded the goal, saying the ball had crossed the line. The Germans were not happy about this decision. Hurst completed his hat trick with a goal in the dying seconds. This was the first ever hat trick in a World Cup final.

What television game were teams from Blackpool and Morecambe the first to take part in?

It's a Knockout

What was the 1960s bicycle which could be stored in the boot of a car?

The *Moulton*

The *Moulton* went into small-scale production earlier in the decade. Alex Moulton of Bradford-on-Avon had designed it to combine compactness, ease of storage and a capability to travel at a speed close to that of a conventional cycle. It was also designed to be ridden easily by either male or female. Raleigh rejected the idea initially, saying they thought the small wheels would never catch on. However the *Moulton* grew in popularity, even encouraging some commuting drivers to use the compact cycle to complete their journey. By 1966, Raleigh had recognized its popularity and bought Moulton's company in the following year.

What colourful book was first read in Brighton in July?

The Yellow Pages

The now familiar *Yellow Pages* were one of several innovations made by the Post Office during the 1960s. The year 1966 also saw the first British Christmas postage stamps. In 1961 the Post Office had begun to install the first pay-on-answer telephone boxes.

What was making life easier for motorists at railway crossings?

The automatic half-barrier

Throughout the 1960s, the new automatic barriers were being installed in place of the old manually opened crossing gates. The period of changeover was accompanied by a campaign of television adverts telling drivers what to do at the new gates. The very first had been installed at Spath near Uttoxeter in 1961. Other changes on the road included the introduction of a new registration system whereby cars' number plates were suffixed with a different letter each year. This was introduced throughout Britain in 1965. The star grading system for petrol was another change introduced over the 1960s, from 1967.

What was Mr Norman Jepson of Sandbach, Cheshire, the winner of on 1 February?

The first £25,000 premium bond prize

Whose figure was 32–22–32?

Twiggy's

With no bust and short hair, Twiggy was a strange candidate for a fashion model. However, during the 1960s, her tube-like figure and shorn hair became all the rage. She did much to popularize the miniskirt. With her Cockney accent and giggly laugh, Twiggy became another image of the 1960s. By the end of the decade she had begun to turn to other things, including records and films. Twiggy's real name was Lesley Hornby, and she was born in Kilburn.

Which comedy duo sang Bring Me Sunshine *at the end of their television shows?*

Morecambe and Wise

Eric and Ernie spent 20 years at the top as television comedy performers. Ernie Wise — the one with short, fat, hairy legs — was the straight man. Eric Morecambe delivered the funny lines, including the catch-phrases, "Get out of that" and "You can't see the join" (a running joke about Ernie's hair being a wig). The duo's shows were enormously popular during the 1960s and 1970s. It became a feature of the shows that 'big-name' actors would make guest appearances in comedy sketches. Glenda Jackson was one such guest. Morecambe and Wise also appeared in three films, but their humour did not adapt well to the big screen. Eric died in 1984.

Who became known for his catch-phrase, "Hello, Good Evening and Welcome"?

David Frost

Frost started his television career as a reporter for *This Week*. He also appeared in *That Was The Week That Was*. He went on to become the central figure in a number of programmes such as *The Frost Report* and *Frost over England*. In recent years he has figured on ITV's breakfast television, where he was their first presenter.

Who set sail this year on a single-handed, round the world voyage aboard his yacht Gipsy Moth IV, *while in his sixties?*

Francis Chichester

What was bombed by the Fleet Air Arm in March?

The *Torrey Canyon*

The *Torrey Canyon* was a 61,000-ton tanker which ran aground between Land's End and the Scilly Isles. It was carrying over 100,000 tons of crude oil and when the vessel broke up thousands of gallons of oil poured towards the Devon and Cornwall coasts. About 70 miles of coastline was polluted in 24 hours. In order to prevent the situation developing into a catastrophe, a flotilla of small ships spread detergent over the spilt oil and planes from the Fleet Air Arm bombed the stricken tanker to set light to the oil remaining. Thanks to these efforts, the damage to the coastline was kept to a minimum, although significant clean-up exercises of beaches and birds were familiar sights on television news.

Who was the surgeon operating on Mr Louis Washkansky on 3 December?

Dr Christiaan Barnard

Mr Washkansky (a 53-year-old grocer) was the recipient of the world's first successful human heart transplant. Barnard carried out the six-hour operation at the Groot Schuur Hospital, Cape Town, South Africa. The heart was transplanted successfully, but Mr Washkansky was to die 18 days later as a result of contracting pneumonia. (Barnard's second transplant patient was to live 20 months, during 1968/9.)

Christiaan Barnard's pioneering surgery led the way for operations which are commonplace today. The 1960s were also to see the first successful liver and lung transplants (in May 1968).

What was first piped ashore at Easington, Humberside on 7 March?

North Sea gas

This gas was from the West Sole field, which 18 months earlier had been the first commercial find in the British part of the North Sea. Since these early days, North Sea gas and oil have become an important part of our lives. Britain's changeover from town gas (coal gas) was to be brought to everyone's attention as gas appliances were converted to use the new source of energy. The human cost of North Sea energy has since been highlighted through drilling rig tragedies.

What became compulsory on all new cars registered in Britain from this year?

Seat belts

What drama series featured Soames and Fleur?

The Forsyte Saga

The Forsyte Saga was based on John Galsworthy's trilogy of novels. It concerned the lives of a London merchant family from 1870 to 1920. Each programme lasted 50 minutes and the series ran for 26 weeks. Soames Forsyte was played by Eric Porter, his wife Irene by Nyree Dawn Porter and their daughter, Fleur, by Susan Hampshire. Kenneth More also featured in the series. *The Forsyte Saga* was the last major British drama series to be filmed entirely in black and white.

Who were Napoleon Solo and Ilya Kuryakin?

The men from UNCLE

The Man From UNCLE was a tremendously popular espionage adventure TV series. Robert Vaughn played Solo and David McCallum Kuryakin. 'UNCLE' stood for United Network Command for Law Enforcement. Their deadly rivals were THRUSH (Technological Hierarchy for the Removal of Undesirables and the Subjection of Humanity). The series was created under the guidance of Ian Fleming, the James Bond author, whose influence is clear in the gadgetry employed in the agents' adventures.

Who became the first UK winner of the Eurovision Song Contest this year?

Sandie Shaw

Sandie won this year's contest with *Puppet On a String* (which also went to number one in the British charts). She had her first number one in 1964, with *Always Something There to Remind Me*. She followed this with hits such as *Girl Don't Come* (1964) and *Long Live Love* (1965). Sandie Shaw was well known for appearing on stage barefoot.

    The UK did not have to wait long for their second Eurovision winner, as Cliff Richard was to win the 1968 contest with *Congratulations*.

Whose wedding to a US master sergeant attracted a television audience of over 20 million?

Elsie Tanner's

What was first blown into just after midnight on 8 October?

The breathalyser

The breathalyser had been invented in America and was used in other countries. The Road Safety Act of 1966 had introduced the breath test and set a limit of 80 milligrams of alcohol in 100cc of blood. It became an offence to drive with a higher level of alcohol content, punishable by a £100 fine and an automatic one-year ban from driving. Although drunk drivers are still with us, the breathalyser has been successful in changing people's social habits. By stopping incapable drivers from getting behind the wheel, it has also saved many lives since its introduction.

Why were zoos closed down and horse racing stopped in 1967?

It was an attempt to control the spread of foot-and-mouth disease

Foot-and-mouth disease was a world-wide problem. Britain had already had some isolated cases, but on 25 October 1967 a farm at Llanyblodwell in Shropshire was hit by the disease. Within four days it had spread to two adjoining farms. Soon the disease was out of control. By mid-November, 80,000 animals had been slaughtered in 21 counties. Restrictions were placed on the movements of animals and people into affected areas. By the end of November all of the United Kingdom (except Northern Ireland) had become a restricted area.

Restrictions affected sport (the RAC motor rally was cancelled) and zoos, such as Whipsnade, were among the places closed down. By March, the outbreak seemed to have been curbed and restrictions were lifted. Altogether there had been a loss of 429,632 animals.

What disappeared from your radio on 29 September?

The BBC Light and Third Programmes and the Home Service

On the following day these made way for the new Radios One, Two, Three and Four. Each station was designed for a specific type of listener. The great days of radio had been left behind as television became the main source of entertainment and news. Over 14 million television licences were issued in 1967. These cost £5 and £5 extra for the new colour televisions. Throughout the 1960s there was still a separate radio licence for those without a television (in 1967 this cost £1 5s).

What was introduced into all British Roman Catholic churches on 3 December?

The English mass

Which football manager announced that he was giving up his successful career to work in television?

Jimmy Hill

After leading Coventry City to the Second Division championship, Hill made this surprise announcement. He had taken the club into Division One for the first time in their history, but decided not to continue his flamboyant managerial career in the top league. He went on to present BBC's *Match of the Day* (amongst other television sports work).

Coventry struggled at first in Division One, but went on to become one of the First Division's most established clubs. They were to defeat Tottenham 3–2 in a memorable Cup Final in 1987.

Which Minister of Transport did not have a driving licence?

Barbara Castle

Labour MP for Blackburn, Barbara Castle was a controversial Minister of Transport from 1965 to 1968. In 1967 she announced that the 70 mph speed limit imposed on motorways would stay. She was also the Transport Minister who announced the introduction of the breathalyser. In 1968 she moved to the Department of Employment and Productivity, remaining controversial with her *In Place of Strife* White Paper, which proposed trade union ballots before strike action.

Who sang The Last Waltz *in 1967?*

Engelbert Humperdinck

After struggling in his early career, Engelbert found success in 1967. His first big hit came with *Release Me* (1967) followed by *There Goes My Everything* and *The Last Waltz* in the same year. By the end of the year he had his own television series and had been at number one for a total of 11 weeks. Humperdinck had several more hits in the decade and attracted a large number of female fans.

Who could talk to the animals?

Dr Doolittle

What happened to the Ronan Point block of flats on 16 May?

A corner of the building collapsed

The Ronan Point collapse took away one entire corner of a new 23-storey block of flats. They collapsed like a pack of cards following a gas explosion on the eighteenth floor. Three people were killed and 80 families made homeless. A fourth victim, an 80-year-old woman, was to die a fortnight later. The flats, in the heart of London's Docklands, were part of a recent slum-clearance contract awarded to Taylor Woodrow–Anglian. They had been occupied for only two months at the time of the collapse. The standard of design and building in such multistorey housing projects obviously provided a 1960s talking-point.

Where were the 1968 Olympic Games held?

Mexico City

The Mexico Games were filled with controversy. Off the track, US athletes gave clenched-fist Black Power salutes during medal ceremonies. In the actual events, Dick Fosbury won the high jump in a totally new style. His head-first, backwards leap became known as the Fosbury Flop. Fellow American Bob Beamon increased the world long jump record by almost two feet. Britain had a thin time in most events, but achieved a great success with David Hemery's victory in the 400 metres hurdles.

What capital city did Russian troops and tanks occupy on 22 August?

Prague

In January 1968, Alexander Dubcek had become the leader of the Czechoslovak Communist Party. Dubcek was a reformer who introduced a number of measures such as a relaxation of press censorship. These developments unsettled Soviet leaders, as they were anxious not to lose an ally state which they regarded as protection against the west. Despite talks between Dubcek and the Russian leaders, Soviet tanks were sent in during August to restore a more pro-Russian regime. Some Czech citizens made demonstrations against this occupation. Many were injured and a number were killed. The most famous of these protests was made by Jan Palach, when he set fire to himself in Wenceslas Square, Prague in January 1969.

What did 13 members of the cast do for a few minutes at the end of the first half of the new rock musical 'Hair', on the day after stage censorship had been abolished?

They performed naked

What musical won this year's Oscar for best film?

Oliver

Based on Dickens' *Oliver Twist*, this film had been developed from a very successful stage show. Music and lyrics were by Lionel Bart. The young Mark Lester played Oliver and Ron Moody was excellent as Fagin. Songs included *Pick A Pocket Or Two*.

Whose enemies included The Joker and Catwoman?

Batman

The Caped Crusader was a fantasy crime fighter who came to Britain in the late 1960s (from the United States of course). Batman and Robin's secret identities, millionaire Bruce Wayne and Dick Grayson, were known only to their butler, Alfred. They lived in the fictional Gotham City where Police Chief O'Hara and Commissioner Gordon called on them to fight equally ridiculous baddies. Young viewers greatly enjoyed Batman's fight sequences when ZAP and SPLAT would be flashed on screen. The heroes travelled to their adventures in the Batmobile which was soon copied by toy manufacturers.

In 1989 a Batman film (with Jack Nicholson as the Joker) was very popular.

Which new television series featured Honolulu detective Steve McGarrett?

Hawaii Five-O

The 1960s saw the start of the television fashion for American police series, a category that also includes *77 Sunset Strip*. Steve McGarrett was rarely seen out of his blue suit and each episode of *Hawaii Five-O* usually ended with him capturing a 'baddie' and saying 'Book 'em Danno' to his sidekick, Danny Williams. The theme tune to the series was very popular and has since been used in 1980s Guinness advertisements.

The fashion for American police television series was to be continued into the 1970s, which would give us *Kojak* and *Columbo*.

Who was Doctor Finlay and Doctor Cameron's housekeeper in Dr Finlay's Casebook?

Janet

What first began to make childbirth less painful in September?

The epidural

This method of relieving pain in childbirth, introduced in the 1960s, involves the injection of anaesthetic into the space around the membrane surrounding the spinal cord. The technique grew in popularity, but some women are wary of this method of pain relief for health reasons.

What did women machinists at Ford's Dagenham and Halewood plants strike for in 1968?

Equal pay

During the 1960s the car industry became a byword for bad industrial relations. Unofficial (wildcat) strikes were common. The year 1966 was an exceptionally bad one, with thousands on strike, laid-off and made redundant in the industry.

The dispute at Dagenham in 1968 is an example of the stand made for equal rights for women over the decade. Women's rights became a topical issue during the 1960s. This dispute cost Ford £9 million. The following year another strike, this one lasting three and a half weeks, also cost the company dearly.

What new types of postage stamps could be bought from 16 September?

First and second class

At the start of the 1960s, the cost of posting a standard letter was 3d. This went up to 4d in 1965. In 1968 the two-tier system came into force, with second class being 4d and first class 5d. The Post Office introduced postcodes in the W1 district of London on 5 June. It also established the National Giro Bank at Bootle on 18 October.

Which new London railway station was opened by the Queen on 14 October?

The new Euston Station

Who was Manchester United's Belfast-born forward who scored their second goal in this year's European cup final?

George Best

Considered by many to be the best ever British footballer, Best made his debut for Manchester United in 1963, aged 17. He was to play more than 450 games for United, scoring nearly 200 goals. His European cup final goal was one of his most important, as it put United ahead in extra time against Benfica. Their eventual 4–1 victory made them the first English team to win the trophy.

Best was a great 1960s sporting figure, helping Manchester United to League championships in 1965 and 1967. His erratic behaviour was to lead to a decline in his career in the 1970s. During the 1980s he even had to serve a spell in prison.

Who had a big hit this year with Those Were the Days?

Mary Hopkin

This Welsh girl with long blonde hair got her big break in 1968, when she appeared on the television talent show, *Opportunity Knocks*. Her success there led to her being recommended to the new Apple record company. Her first record for the company, and her biggest success, was *Those Were the Days*. Mary Hopkin's period of success was limited to the end of the decade. She was to sing the 1970 UK entry for the Eurovision Song Contest, *Knock, Knock, Who's There?*

Which Irish comedian ended his show with the words "Goodnight, good luck and may your God go with you"?

Dave Allen

Dave Allen's style was very simple. He sat casually on a high stool and rattled off gags to his audience, pausing only for a sip of whisky or a drag on his cigarette. Religion and politics were the subjects of many of his jokes, despite his having been brought up in a devout Roman Catholic family.

Who was the great West Indian cricketer who scored six sixes off one over, bowled by Glamorgan bowler Malcolm Nash in August?

Gary Sobers

Who took a giant leap for mankind on 21 July?

Neil Armstrong on the first moon walk

At the start of the 1960s man made his first space flight and the end of the decade saw the first landing on the moon by a manned craft. Apollo 11 blasted off from Cape Kennedy on 16 July. On board were Armstrong, Buzz Aldrin and Michael Collins. Four days later, the Eagle module landed on the moon's surface. Watched by hundreds of millions on their television sets, Armstrong first set foot on the moon's surface at 3.56am on 21 July. His first words were, "That's one small step for man, one giant leap for mankind." This became one of the great quotes of the 1960s. Armstrong and Aldrin carried out a series of experiments on the moon's surface, as well as planting the Stars and Stripes.

What made its maiden flight on 9 April?

The British prototype of Concorde

The first supersonic passenger airliner was an Anglo-French project. The French version had made its first flight in March. People were fascinated by Concorde's unusual design, especially its swept-back wings and moveable nose. When Concorde landed at Heathrow for the first time there were many complaints about the noise. Concorde was capable of crossing the Atlantic in half the normal time. It eventually went into service in 1976, 16 years after plans for a supersonic airliner had been announced and after an enormous amount of money had been spent on the project.

From where did President Nixon begin to withdraw American soldiers in 1969?

Vietnam

After the defeat of the French, Vietnam had been split in two, with a Communist North and a Republic of South Vietnam. By 1959 North and South were fighting. In 1961 significant American involvement began with the sending of some 2,000 servicemen to help South Vietnam. As the war went on, the scale of American involvement grew, until April 1969, when there were 543,400 US servicemen in Vietnam. Nixon had been elected in 1968, with a commitment to starting a withdrawal from Vietnam. American involvement in the war ended in the early 1970s.

What tiny Caribbean island was invaded by a small force of British marines in March (the troops soon being replaced by 40 police constables)?

Anguilla

Who had a hit record this year with Two Little Boys?

Rolf Harris

This was Harris's biggest hit and the last number one record of the 1960s. Rolf Harris was a popular television entertainer who made great play of his Australian background. Familiar songs on his television show were *Tie Me Kangaroo Down, Sport* and *Sun Arise*, which he accompanied with his famous wobble board. He was famous for his high-speed paintings, which he used to introduce songs on his show. The bearded and bespectacled Australian also brought us the three-legged Jake in the comedy song *Jake the Peg*.

Which children's programme featured Dougal and Florence?

The Magic Roundabout

This children's television series had been introduced by the BBC in 1964 and ran all through the 1960s and on until 1977. The characters of Florence and Dougal, the mop-headed dog, were accompanied by Dylan (a guitar-playing rabbit), Brian the snail and Ermintrude the cow. Also familiar to *Magic Roundabout* viewers is Zebedee, who bounced about the garden, going "Boing!".

Whose mission was 'to boldly go where no man has gone before'?

The starship Enterprise in *Star Trek*

This science fiction television show featured the adventures of the Enterprise and its crew, which included Captain James T Kirk, Mr Spock (First Officer), Scotty, Sulu, Chekov and Uhura. The lead characters were Kirk and Spock, played by William Shatner and Leonard Nimoy. Mr Spock was half human and half Vulcan. He had pointed ears, green blood, was telepathic and emotionless. He also had a logical explanation for everything. Though made and first shown in the late 1960s, *Star Trek* was to achieve its enormous popularity in the 1970s. A number of expensive *Star Trek* movies were also to be made.

Who featured as the Roman slave, Lurcio, in the comedy series Up Pompeii?

Frankie Howerd

What coin went out of circulation in August?

The old halfpenny

During the 1960s, Britain still used pounds, shillings and pence. Decimalization Day was not to be until 15 February 1971. However the introduction of new decimal coins started in the 1960s, as we prepared for the changeover to the decimal system. The first announcement of the changeover was made in 1966 and the first new coins to be introduced were the five- and ten-pence pieces, in April 1968. The old halfpenny disappeared in August 1969 and the seven-sided 50-pence piece came into circulation in October. This was the eventual replacement for the brown ten bob note.

What increasing problem did Glasgow Rangers Football Club announce plans to combat during this year?

Football hooliganism

Serious football hooliganism was a product of the 1960s which was to continue into the 1970s and 1980s. Many people compared the trouble at grounds with the good behaviour of football's (much larger) crowds in the 1930s and 1950s. Rangers' planned precautions included the banning of convicted troublemakers and measures to stop people bringing alcohol into the ground.

In March 1969, soccer hooligans ran riot on London's Underground, causing thousands of pounds' worth of damage. The problem remains but has lessened, though only at the cost of a heavy police presence at games and the segregation or even banning of away supporters.

What began on BBC1 and ITV on 14 November?

Colour broadcasting

BBC2 had begun the first colour broadcasting in July 1967. The first seven hours were mostly devoted to coverage of Wimbledon. While 1969 saw the extension of colour broadcasting, it was still only available to a small minority. Of 15,496,061 licences sold in 1969, only 99,419 were for colour. The most effective restriction on colour television was its cost. A 19-inch colour set would cost approximately £290 at the end of the decade. When considered in relation to an average (manual) wage of £24 16s a week, this is seen to be much more expensive than today. Supply and demand, together with technical development, would change this situation so that, by 1988, of 19,354,442 licences, 17,133,960 were for colour. The 1960s were effectively a black and white decade for television, but they set in motion the inevitable takeover of the colour set.

In what way was the minimum voting age changed by this year's Representation of the People Act?

It was reduced from 21 to 18

Whose wife was a silly old moo and son-in-law a long-haired Scouse git?

Alf Garnett's

Warren Mitchell played Alf, the unlikely star of the television comedy series, *Till Death Us Do Part*. Alf Garnett was a loud, self-opinionated little man who spent his time expressing his (usually very poor) opinion of practically everyone and everything. Only the Queen, Winston Churchill and West Ham United were safe from his criticisms. Alf spent much of his time arguing with his son-in-law, Mike, who was married to his daughter Rita (played by Una Stubbs). Alf's long-suffering wife, Else, was played by Dandy Nichols. At the time the series brought many complaints about bad language and blasphemy, but it was also popular and many more people enjoyed laughing at Alf's views on the world.

What did Prince Charles become on 1 July at Caernarfon Castle?

The nineteenth Prince of Wales

Most Welsh people looked forward to the ceremony, but a small minority of Nationalists considered it an insult to Wales and security was tight. A mock bomb was found on a railway bridge over the River Dee which the royal train was due to cross. During the day's ceremony, an egg-throwing incident and a banana skin thrown under a horse added sour notes. Despite this, some 250,000 people crowded into Caernarfon to view the Investiture and millions more watched world-wide on television.

Who were the twin brothers who appeared at the Old Bailey in March and were given long prison sentences for murder?

Ronnie and Reggie Kray

The Kray twins were vicious and violent criminals who organized Soho protection rackets. Together with their elder brother, Charles, they had long histories of criminal activity over the 1950s and 1960s, but the police had experienced difficulty in obtaining the witnesses and evidence needed for a conviction. The Kray twins had attracted a certain amount of criminal glamour to themselves, sometimes mixing with showbusiness figures. When they came to trial in 1969 there was a significant media interest. They were charged with murdering Jack 'The Hat' McVitie and George Cornell. The Kray twins were found guilty and received the longest sentences ever imposed for murder at the Old Bailey: they were jailed for life, with a recommendation that they serve at least 30 years.

Who had long hair, a hooked nose, a falsetto singing voice, played the ukulele and made a record of Tiptoe Through the Tulips?

Tiny Tim